GETTING
RUSSIA
RIGHT

D0973732

GETTING RUSSIA RIGHT

DMITRI V. TRENIN

CARNEGIE ENDOWMENT

FOR INTERNATIONAL PEACE

WASHINGTON DC · MOSCOW · BEIJING · BEIRUT · BRUSSELS

© 2007 Carnegie Endowment for International Peace.

Carnegie Endowment for International Peace
1779 Massachusetts Avenue, N.W.
Washington, D.C. 20036
202-483-7600, Fax 202-483-1840
www.CarnegieEndowment.org

The Carnegie Endowment for International Peace normally does not take institutional positions on public policy issues; the views and recommendations presented in this publication do not necessarily represent the views of the Carnegie Endowment, its officers, staff, or trustees.

Typesetting by Stephen McDougal
Printed by United Book Press

Library of Congress Cataloging-in-Publication Data

Trenin, Dmitri.
  Getting Russia right / by Dmitri Trenin.
    p. cm.
  Includes index.
  ISBN 978-0-87003-234-9—ISBN 978-0-87003-235-6 1. United States—Foreign relations—Russia (Federation) 2. Russia (Federation)—Foreign relations—United States. 3. European Union countries—Foreign relations—Russia (Federation). 4. Russia (Federation)—Foreign relations—European Union countries. I. Title.

  JZ1480.A57R879 2007
  327.73047—dc22   200702614

12 11 10 09 08 07   12345   1st Printing 2007

For Vera

CONTENTS

FOREWORD

AMBASSADOR
JAMES F. COLLINS

Dmitri Trenin's latest volume is a welcome tonic for those who believe Russia's relations with the United States and Europe need a fresh approach. In this essay the author undertakes a personal quest to answer the question of why Russia's relations with the United States and Europe have soured in the last decade, and what can be done to recover the hope and promise that accompanied the end of the Cold War and dissolution of the USSR. The result is essential reading for policy officials, opinion leaders, and the public at large concerned to assure Russia a constructive place in the future world order and to see its relations with the United States and Europe develop in a positive direction.

Trenin is a thoughtful student of Russia's history, its relations with the outside world, and its transition from communism. He brings an intellectually rigorous perspective to his subject, and he has carefully thought out conclusions that will be both controversial and in some cases unacceptable for many in his own country and in the West. At the core of Trenin's work lies a fundamental challenge to readers. He asks them to put aside preconceived ideas about his native Russia and to explore the Russia of today with a fresh eye. He argues that today's often cliché-ridden portrayal of Russia in American and European media and political debate is based not on a realistic understanding of what has happened to his country over the past fifteen years, but on a misreading of Russia's capacities, historical traditions, and present realities. This distortion of Russian reality, with its persistent reversion to old stereotypes, leads to both bad policy and a negative dynamic in Russia's relations with the West that threatens Russian as well as Western interests.

In summoning his readers to reform and rationalize their thinking about Russia, Trenin is hard-headed and realistic about his own nation. His coldly clinical analysis of Russia's political, economic, and social system pulls no punches. He describes the Putin political system as more akin to czarism than a modern, functioning democratic state. And he makes clear that the Russian elite's misconceptions about the outside world, especially the United States and Europe, are dangerous for Russian interests. Nevertheless, Trenin makes the fundamental point that Russia has traversed tremendous distance along a path of development that if pursued holds the prospect of a democratic future. He sees three key developments that have fundamentally changed the Russia of the past and set it on a course toward Westernization. They are the emergence for the first time in Russia's history of a capitalist economy based on western concepts of private property; the unprecedented opening of Russia to the outside world; and, with the end of the Russian empire, the beginning of development of Russia as a modern nation state. These three features of post-Soviet Russia, Trenin argues, have not only changed the economic model in Russia, but have fundamentally altered the ideology and way of thinking that is shaping Russia's institutional development, relations with the outside world, and definition of Russia as a nation. It is at the core of what he describes as the path Russia's "first free generation" is taking to make their country and society "Western" and bringing it to become a "land of capitalism and private interest."

In the remaining chapters of this essay Trenin builds a case for the need to replace present U.S. and European thinking about Russia as a failed experiment in transition to western democracy with a model that can take advantage of the positive potential the changes he has described represent for Russia's future. As background Trenin offers a historical review of Russia's relations with the West. He notes that Russians draw a distinction between becoming "western," in the sense of transforming their country through a process Trenin equates with "capitalist modernization," and transforming Russia through the country's absorption— either literally or figuratively—by the West or its defining institutions of

NATO and the EU. He concludes that while the former has traction among Russians who see their society as European by culture, tradition, and affinity, the latter involves an unacceptable merging of Russia and Europe in a way that Russia has resisted from the very beginning of its existence, a process Trenin sees in any case as beyond Russia's capacity and the limits of Europe's institutions. In sum, he believes Russia has embarked on the path of capitalist modernization to become western but, like many other nations outside Europe, will resist imposition of models from the "Old West," the world of "Old Europe," as a prototype. Rather, Russia is best seen as becoming a part of what Trenin calls the "New West," the complex of nations moving along a path of transformation based on a capitalist market system and private property.

Looking at Russia in this way, Trenin argues, opens the possibility for more realistic analysis of Russia's development and makes the case for adopting a "new paradigm" for Russia in the West that can support more stable and productive Russia–West relations. That paradigm, Trenin argues, has to start with objective analysis. It needs to look dispassionately at Russian reality and realistically assess Russia's importance to effective global governance. Trenin notes that the United States and Europe are still looking at Russia in terms of the 1990s and applying the "democracy paradigm" to it. This has become counterproductive to Western and Russian interests and an obstacle to the development of positive working relations between the West and Russia. More productive in Trenin's view would be an approach that focuses on opportunities that emerge from viewing Russia as part of what he terms the "New West in potential," the complex of countries like Brazil, India, Argentina, Indonesia, and China, which, in the aftermath of the Cold War, have opted for a capitalist path if not yet for democracy. Russia is on the way to joining this club, and a paradigm that takes Russia as such would make possible more rational assessment of opportunities for cooperation bilaterally and multilaterally and would open the way to take advantage of common imperatives of a capitalist system that the New and Old West share.

Trenin concludes that adoption of a new paradigm for Russia's relations with the United States and Europe can serve long-term Western, Russian, and global interests. He believes that Russia, with its emerging capitalist society motivated by economic and political self-interest, is likely to cooperate in addressing pressing global issues such as terrorism, global warming, proliferation of WMD, and energy security. That cooperation will depend, however, on whether Europe and the

United States take account of Russian interests and respect its status as a major power, including in institutions like the G8 and the United Nations. At the same time Trenin calls on the United States and Europe to continue working to strengthen the forces of liberalism and modernization in Russia. Russia should be held to account for its actions by institutions where its membership requires respect for defined rules of the road. Bringing Russia into organizations such as the WTO and encouraging respect for property rights and rules of international commerce can further promote the rule of law and Russian behavior consistent with internationally defined norms. He also believes that backing progressive reforms in the states of the former Soviet Union can support and strengthen the forces for positive change in Russia. All this will probably not spare Trenin criticism for seeming to downgrade the priority accorded democracy promotion, rule of law, and human rights. The proponents of the democracy paradigm will almost certainly see retreat where Trenin advocates reason and rationality. However, his call for the United States and Europe to take a pragmatic view of possibilities regarding Russia offers a much needed fresh approach with a well argued outcome that holds the possibility of melding the priorities of support for democracy with the needs for enlisting Russia in global coopera-tion. If the United States and Europe begin to see Russia as an emerging capitalist society rather than a failed democratic polity, Trenin believes that Russia will respond, and the result can be a more predictable and productive future for Russia's relations with Washington and Europe's capitals. With that objective foremost, *Getting Russia Right* will command attention and respect.

James F. Collins

Senior Associate and Director, Russian and Eurasian Program; Diplomat in Residence

Carnegie Endowment for International Peace

ACKNOWLEDGMENTS

In writing this book, I was very fortunate to rely on the advice and insights of several outstanding people. George Perkovich, Vice President for Studies at the Carnegie Endowment, first encouraged me to write a short essay to summarize some of the key ideas about Russia's past, present, and future. In this, he provided a useful framework and a powerful impetus for my thinking and writing. Later, he also offered thoughtful comments and observations on the initial draft. Professor Angela Stent of Georgetown University, one of the world's foremost experts on Russia and its policies, thoroughly reviewed and critiqued the text and suggested practical ways to improve it. Further, I am deeply thankful to James F. Collins, U.S. Ambassador to Russia (1998–2001) for agreeing to write a foreword to the book, and to my Carnegie colleague and Endowment Vice President for Studies, Mark Medish, for his most useful comments. In particular, I am indebted to Stephen Minikes, former U.S. Ambassador to the OSCE in Vienna, who took a keen interest in the subject and put my text to most close scrutiny. I am also grateful to Strobe Talbott for reading the text and offering valuable suggestions.

I am most appreciative of the professional support and excellent advice of the Carnegie publications staff, without whom the manuscript would not have made it to book form. Carrie Mullen, Ilonka Oszvald, and Tina Wong Coffron were my patient and resourceful guides along that journey. Peter Slavin, the editor, made me think harder not merely about the usage of words in a language that is not my native tongue, but also about some of the concepts behind them.

I am also grateful for the generous support of the Carnegie Corporation of New York and the Charles Stewart Mott Foundation for the Carnegie Moscow Center.

Although the book was conceived, conceptualized, and partially written in Russia, I profited enormously from the opportunity to spend nine months during 2006–2007 in Washington, D.C., where the project was finalized. For this, I am most thankful to Jessica T. Mathews, President of the Carnegie Endowment for International Peace, and Paul Balaran, the Endowment's Executive Vice President, whose idea it was for me to leave the hustle and bustle of Moscow and spend time in the relative quiet of Washington.

Finally, I want to thank my wife, Vera, for her patience, tolerance, and cheerfulness that allow me to pursue my research interests while keeping our lives whole and full.

INTRODUCTION

The idea of this essay was born out of frustration, rather than inspiration. Inspiration came later. The starting thought was why the country that, just a decade and a half ago, was hailed as an emerging market democracy, a returnee, at long last, to a Europe whole and free, and a strategic partner of the United States, had sunk so low in the opinion of most in the West that China's current "socialism with a market face" wins hands down in almost any comparison.

True, Russia's transition has been troubled almost from the beginning. Relatively few in the West recoiled at the armed violence of the 1993 Moscow standoff between President Boris Yeltsin and the Supreme Soviet, but many were astounded by the huge gains by the nationalists in the first democratic elections to the new parliament two and a half months later. A great many more were appalled by the brutalities of the war in Chechnya, begun in 1994. Yeltsin's re-election in 1996, despite the way it was achieved, brought a sigh of relief, but Yeltsin's failing health and the rise of the oligarchy symbolized the morass into which Russia had strayed. The 1998 financial default came almost as a coup de grâce: Russia was *lost in transition*, and the only question debated was who was responsible.

Miraculously, as Russia started to rebound, buoyed by high oil prices and state stabilization efforts, new hopes were born. Western pundits and politicians discovered a glint of modernization in the approach taken by Vladimir Putin, who succeeded Yeltsin a few hours before the advent of the year 2000. At the same time, the new president made it clear that his first priority was to stabilize the country, which had been in turmoil ever since Gorbachev's perestroika cut at the roots of the Soviet communist system. Stabilization took the familiar form of recentralization of power, which fueled suspicions of a rollback of new freedoms. A common joke in Moscow in the spring of 2000 was that the new president had zeroed in on a Korean model for Russia, but had yet to decide *which* Korean model to follow, that of the North or the South.

That was no more than a joke which told more of the people passing it around than about its message. Putin's early reforms (taxation, land, administration, pensions, education, utilities, and so on), many of which were incomplete or struggling, created a new opening in the country's domestic evolution. His sobriety and healthy pragmatism were in sharp contrast with the practices of his predecessor. After 9/11, Putin's instant support for the United States, his full embrace of the U.S. military operation in Afghanistan, and his willingness not to oppose the introduction of American military forces into former Soviet Central Asia, were all impressive. Putin's October 2001 speech in the Bundestag, delivered in German, sounded like a manifesto of Russia's European vocation.

The new era of universal good will was short-lived. 2002 was a year of missed opportunities, both between Russia and the United States and Russia and the European Union (EU). Strategic partnerships were proclaimed, but never carried out. In 2003, Russia opposed the U.S. invasion of Iraq—in part because Washington failed to understand Moscow's interests, and in part due to the opportunistic idea of starting a new entente with France and Germany. Domestically, the jailing of Mikhail Khodorkovsky and the destruction of his YUKOS business empire marked a watershed. Toward the end of 2003, the two parties recognized in the West as democratic lost all their seats in the Russian parliament.

Putin's second term opened in 2004 with the tragedy of a terrorist attack in Beslan, resulting in the deaths of 333 students and teachers. His response was a further centralization of power. Even as these political reforms were branded antidemocratic, Putin, in an astonishing statement that apparently came from the heart, accused the West of a desire to weaken and dismember Russia and of using the terrorists for that purpose. The Ukrainian presidential elections, culminating in the fall of 2004 in an Orange Revolution, further poisoned the Russian–Western relationship, but helped the Kremlin to complete its turnaround in foreign policy.

In a word, Russia, previously a Pluto in the Western solar system, has spun out of its orbit and gone into a trajectory of its own, powered by a determination to found its own system. The former Soviet borderlands, newly independent, became a focus of Moscow's policy for the first time. Russia sided with China within the rapidly rising Shanghai Cooperation Organization in calling for U.S. military withdrawal from Central Asia, and it managed to win back Uzbekistan, an estranged former U.S. ally in the region.

Having proclaimed itself an energy superpower, Russia in 2005 canceled gas price subsidies to the new states and went ahead toward a showdown with the largest of them, Ukraine. It did not shy away from shutting off gas supplies to Ukraine until the latter agreed to new prices. Russia then indicated its readiness to rethink the solution to the frozen conflicts in Georgia and Moldova along the lines of the Kosovo model, i.e., full independence for the separatist enclaves. The fact that Ukraine, Georgia, and Moldova are all led by pro-Western governments was not lost on anyone. Moscow's strong-arm methods in dealing with them led to accusations that Russia was employing the "energy weapon" to punish them for their foreign policy. The fact that similar treatment was meted out in 2007 to dictatorial and supposedly pro-Moscow Belarus was attributed to Russia's desire to annex that country or at least to fully dominate it economically.

Within Russia itself, "sovereignty" became the favorite buzzword with senior government officials and their political allies. The idea of making the country impervious to political influence from abroad was enshrined in the law governing the activities of nongovernmental organizations (NGOs), which had been originally conceived by the security services in the wake of the "color revolutions" and had become effective in 2006. The killing in Moscow of a top investigative journalist, Anna Politkovskaya, and the poisoning by polonium of a former security officer, Alexander Litvinenko, in London helped build an image of a country where security services reign supreme, free to eliminate the Kremlin's enemies at will.

Russia not only refused to join the United States and the EU countries in imposing harsh sanctions against Iran at the United Nations, after

Tehran persisted in its unabated nuclear program and took an abrasive and provocative public stance. Moscow also sold Iran antiaircraft missile systems. Commenting on U.S. policies in the Middle East, Russian foreign minister Sergey Lavrov repeatedly said his country would not be drawn into a confrontation between civilizations. Russia would not take sides, but would follow its own interests. The crescendo came, on the Russian side, when President Putin descended on the Munich security conference in February 2007 to personally deliver a scathing and totally undiplomatic criticism of U.S. foreign policy

These and other events led a number of Western observers to conclude that Russia had departed from the path of democracy and gone back to its authoritarian tradition. In descriptions of the Russian domestic scene, *Back in the USSR* or, at least, *Welcome to the Soviet Union 2.0* became a common conclusion. In terms of foreign policy, "neoimperialism" was the most-often heard charge: Russia was using its energy abundance as a weapon and applied economic sanctions to punish Western-leaning young democracies, such as Georgia. The regional bully in Eurasia, my longtime colleague Andrew Kuchins said wryly, was issuing a new battle cry: *Authoritarians of the world, unite!*

The Kremlin managed to withstand the barrage of unprecedented criticism and controversy that accompanied its chairmanship of the G8. In July 2006, it hosted the summit in St. Petersburg without giving an inch to its critics and would-be detractors. The Kremlin took a hard line toward the European Union and read the riot act to its new members, which included Poland and Estonia. It berated its longtime darling, the Organization for Security and Co-operation in Europe (OSCE), for focusing too much on elections in the post-Soviet republics and indicated that its interest in the Council of Europe and the European Court of Human Rights was waning.

The Russian leadership has definitely found a new confidence and established a new paradigm for dealing with the West, while the West has not created a new one for dealing with Russia. Obviously, the principles, incentives, and sanctions developed in the 1990s no longer apply. But what should the new paradigm look like? Should it be a new containment policy, as some propose? Or, more robustly, a rollback of Russia's new influence? Or even regime change in Russia itself?

To be able to formulate a new policy course, one needs to take a closer, harder, and longer look at the country in question. Is it really going in the wrong direction, sliding back ever faster and becoming a threat-in-waiting, or is it moving along and even forward in a familiar pattern of two steps forward, one-and-a-half-steps back? Or is it something else, something nonlinear?

While the interest in Russian affairs has slackened considerably in comparison to both Soviet times and the heady 1990s, there is no shortage of publications on contemporary Russia. Even a cursory analysis reveals that they focus heavily on Russian politics. It is astounding but also telling that a long list of books bear a similar title, *Putin's Russia*. As the title suggests, their authors frankly focus on Kremlin power and Kremlin politics.

There is nothing wrong with that. Political leadership remains tremendously important in Russia, and little of anything significant in Russian politics today can be achieved without the Kremlin, much less against it. However, since the advent of the twenty-first century, politics, while still dominant, has become the least dynamic part of the Russian picture. This is not where promising beginnings are happening, or a new wave of democratic change is rising. Yet, there is a Russia beyond Putin's, and it stretches far and wide outside the long shadows of the Kremlin towers. This Russia, a land of capitalism and private interest, will be our first way station toward finding an answer to the question of Western policy.

The second station, or chapter, will deal with the phenomenon of the West. It will study the main stages of its evolution and seek to define its meaning at the beginning of the twenty-first century. The key issues here are Westernization and Western integration. This will be important as we proceed to compare Russia to others, those who have made themselves part of the West, and those who are now in the process of modernizing their institutions to become Western. Comparisons can be very helpful, both when they are contemporary vis-à-vis other post-communist countries and when they are historical vis-à-vis Western countries at various stages of their development.

Distinguishing between institutionally Western and politically (or strategically) pro-Western, the third chapter will look at Russia's own policy toward the West. A discussion of the country's identity and its ever-changing historical attitudes toward Western Europe and later North America will precede the analysis of Moscow's relations with the West since the breakup of the Soviet Union.

Drawing the lessons from U.S. and EU policies toward the Russian Federation will be the mission of chapter four, a companion to its predecessor. This will seek to yield part of the answer to the question, "What Went Wrong?" Finally, the conclusion will attempt to lay out a new paradigm for Russia's relations with America and Europe in the early part of the twenty-first century. Ten or fifteen years from now, are we headed toward a new confrontation, a belated second stage of the half-century-old conflict, or some new era of interaction, competitive for sure, but increasingly integrative?

Finally and inevitably, one has to squarely deal with the question, "Does Russia matter?" In other words, will the things this short book sets out to discuss make any big difference? To quite a few, post-Soviet Russia continues to be irrelevant, except for its capacity to make occasional mischief. It is believed to be a declining power that has just entered the third decade of downward slide. The current rise of the Kremlin is thought to be merely the function of exceptionally high energy prices, which will fall, sooner or later, cutting Russia down to its right size. Russia's true size, according to this school of thought, is determined by its dwindling population, the deteriorating health of its people, its inability to innovate, and its incompetence at keeping together a vast territory which lies between the world's richest region, Europe, its most dynamic area, Northeast Asia, and its most turbulent neighborhood, the Greater Middle East.

This view mistakes reconfiguration for decline. It fails to give credit to the Russians for their resilience despite the loss of a state, their economic and value systems, and their capacity to move on. It prefers to focus on the old, like the KGB and its successor, the FSB, which is familiar, if reprehensible, rather than on the new, which has been emerging since the liberation of the private interest. Russia is coming back, but not as an archaic empire. It is becoming a qualitatively new actor, an economic and a cultural force, rather than simply a military power, a competitor rather than an opponent. Russia is no longer "the Other." In pursuit of its interests, it is increasingly dealing with the West on the West's own terms, primarily through the use of economic instruments in a globalized world.

This could be the unsettling thing. It might help explain the difference between America's and Europe's approaches to Russia and China. However, understanding Russia is critical for Western policy makers. In its post-Iraq foreign policy, a new U.S. administration, whether Democratic or Republican, will have to face up to the need to rebuild relationships with the world's key players. Attempts at reconstituting the West as a union of democracies, no matter how successful, will be woefully insufficient for ensuring global governance, the natural primary foreign policy task for an enlightened American leadership. As for Europe, sorting out its relationship with Russia would help it define its geographical boundaries and its global strategy.

In order to set out a credible and long-term Russia policy, the United States and Europe need a set of new first principles about Russia. The two rival approaches of today—pretending that things are not so bad versus protesting that they, in fact, are—are not working. Threats to throw Russia out of the G8 and treat it as a renegade show frustration, but they do not offer a new and better way forward. An analysis of Russian social and economic trends should illuminate the future. Russia is probably not going to *join* the West, but it is on a long march to *become* Western, "European," and capitalist, even if not for a long while democratic. I mean European in terms of civilization rather than part of the European Union, and gradually more Western rather than pro-Western (or pro-American). Russia will matter in the foreseeable future, and that is why it is important to read it right.

CHAPTER 1

THE RUSSIA
BEYOND PUTIN'S RUSSIA

Russia has a reputation of being a land of extremes. Even analysis of Russia could suffer from that affliction. In the last two decades, many inside players and outside observers hoped that Russia would change not only profoundly, but, in effect overnight. These overoptimistic expectations were soon dashed, only to be replaced with deep disillusionment and pessimism about Russia.

As Russia enters the 2007–2008 election cycle, there is no question that it has a czarist political system, in which all major decisions are taken by one institution, the presidency, also known as the Kremlin. The separation of powers, provided for under the 1993 constitution, is a fiction. All institutions of the federal government, from the cabinet to the bicameral legislature, are in reality mere agents of the presidency. The legal system is anything but independent, especially when dealing with the opponents of the Kremlin, and the prosecutor general's office has become a tool of choice in the hands of the presidency. Officially known as a federation, Russia is in reality closer to a unitary state, with the governors of the country's seven dozen regions appointed and dismissed by the president.

The party system is represented by the principal, alternative parties in power (United Russia and A Just Russia), flanked by loyal fellow travelers, such as the right-wing nationalist Liberal Democratic Party of Vladimir Zhirinovsky; the communist opposition is genuine, but much reduced. The democratic and liberal parties, Yabloko (The Russian Democratic Party) and the Union of Right Forces (SPS), with no seats in parliament, have become marginalized. The entrance bar to the state Duma, the lower house of parliament, is set at 7 percent, which makes it prohibitive for any political groups that are not part of the Kremlin-designed system.

The Kremlin controls, directly or indirectly, virtually all the national electronic media, especially television, and wields growing influence over print media. The amount of official information released to the media is based on the Kremlin's notion of what the public at large needs to know. Leaks, so frequent under Yeltsin, have become a rarity. Even some of Putin's most important decisions come as surprises, and the reasons for them are likely to remain mystery, at least so long as he is president.

The issue of succession at the Kremlin is vital for this kind of political system. The stakes are extremely high, especially for those in direct proximity to the Kremlin chief, some of whom are likely to benefit from his successor, while others are likely to lose even more than their formal positions and official remuneration would suggest.

The oligarchs, business tycoons who kept the government at their beck and call under Yeltsin, are gone as a group—three exiled, two in jail, and others surviving as wealthy individuals rather than all-powerful courtiers. By contrast, some of the key figures of the Putin presidency are entrusted with supervising the most profitable sectors of the national economy, namely oil and gas and the arms trade. High-ranking jobs with the government have become springboards to rapid self-enrichment. Today's Russia is probably ruled by the richest group of individuals anywhere in the world. It would not be much of an exaggeration to say that Russia is run and largely owned by the same people.

The degree of corruption in Russia is difficult to gauge. Georgi Satarov, Yeltsin's former political adviser and now president of INDEM, a think tank, has presented a study claiming that the "corruption tax," which businesses and citizens have to bear, could be as high as $356 billion per year. Sergei Guriev, rector of the Russian Economic School, says that the level of corruption in Russia is 40 percent higher than it should be for a country at its stage of development.

The difference could reflect Russia's richness in oil and gas wealth. To some, it is nothing but an oil curse, which threatens to turn the country into a petrostate. If this happens, it will be above all, as Lilia Shevtsova notes, the failure of the country's ruling elite, whose many members are greedy, rapacious, and totally indifferent to the situation of their compatriots.

Kremlin ideologues and propagandists generally do not deny that these problems exist, but they argue that they are widely shared around the world. Their preferred line is that no one is perfect. There is no ideal democracy, no absolutely clean government, no responsible statesman who is not grooming a successor, and so on. And, to quote another favorite maxim dating back to the nineteenth century, the only true European in Russia is the government. His Imperial Majesty's Government, one is tempted to add.

This is where most analysts and observers make a full stop. This book ventures further. It broadly agrees with the critics' analysis and rejects defense of the status quo as obviously self-serving. However, it seeks to go beyond the usual policy discourse in its search for the factors and forces that are capable of pushing Russia forward. It also attempts to look into the new realities already created by those forces and assess their potential for maintaining the pace of change. In a way, it is a journey into a Russia beyond Putin's Russia.

What Moves Russia Forward?

Today's Russia is different from the Soviet Union in so many ways that the idea of a *USSR Version 2.0* would seem preposterous to any objective observer in Russia. Of the things that have brought about that irreversible change, two stand out. One is money, which has become virtually the center of everything in today's Russia. The other one is Russia's openness to the outside world.

Money

The lasting change in Russia at the turn of the 1990s was not the advent of democracy, but the introduction and institutionalization of money and of everything it brings with it. Ever since the New Economic Policy had been phased out in the late 1920s, together with gold and silver coins, the Soviet Union had been a country which had no use for *real* money. Of course, ruble notes were duly printed and national budgets regularly approved, but central to the Soviet economy was the allocation of nonmonetary resources. All property was owned by the state, which also treated people as its property. Prices were set and changed arbitrarily.

This included the ruble's exchange rate. After World War II, Stalin made his economists and financiers figure out the ruble to the dollar ratio, using all the comparative data available to them. They came up with a 14:1 rate, which they considered moderately favorable to the Soviet currency unit. Stalin still did not like the result and erased the "1." From then on, it was 4:1. When Khrushchev carried out his currency reform in 1961, 1 new ruble (equal to 10 "Stalin" ones) was officially (and quite arbitrarily) set at $1.11.

This, of course, mainly applied to foreigners, for ordinary Soviet citizens were not allowed to own foreign exchange, and any operations with it were punishable by several years in prison. Not everyone knew, however, what foreign money looked like. The following is a true story: In the 1970s, police officers in Kazan, a major Soviet city, found a stack of U.S. dollars in a criminal's apartment and failed to confiscate it, because they considered them ancient notes. No sooner had these restrictions been abolished in 1991 than currency exchange offices started to dot the streets of all Russian cities.

Not trusting the rapidly depreciating ruble, ordinary people started saving dollars. As a hedge against runaway inflation, all prices, from cars to restaurant menus to defense spending to meager salaries and pensions, began to be quoted in dollars. A 1990s joke had a Russian, who has just returned from a trip to America, tell his friend in amazement: "Over there, they are using our bucks, *baksy*, too!" For more than a decade, the ruble was reduced to the role of a tender for small purchases, a humble subunit of the dollar with an ever-falling value. A headline in a Moscow paper in the 1990s proclaimed, "The ruble is not worth a cent . . . and soon it won't be worth a pfennig." People had more or fewer rubles (or dollars, marks, etc.) in their hands, but what they had was real money.

In 1998, the ruble, which had just been stabilized, was sharply devalued, its value in dollar terms shrinking four times in almost as many days. By 2006, however, the Russian currency had made a spectacular comeback. Not only has it been able to fully restore the postdefault balance against the dollar (26:1), but it has been gaining 10 percent in real value every year. The much-ridiculed and yet approved bill passed by the Duma banned, under the penalty of a symbolic fine, the use of the names of foreign currency units in quoting prices, expenses, and so forth in Russia. More seriously, starting in mid-2006, the ruble became almost fully convertible inside the country. Long lampooned and seldom trusted, the ruble has become real money and even the preferred currency. Salaries denominated in rubles work to better advantage for their recipients than those still quoted in dollars.

Private Property

Money, however, is merely a precursor and agent of the really fundamental change, which had to do with private property. From the days of the later grand dukes of Moscow, the ruler of the Kremlin had been the supreme owner of all property in his land, starting with land itself and extending to its residents' lives. This clearly set Russia apart from Western Europe. This situation did not change until Catherine the Great's 1785 charter to the Russian nobility, which at last turned them into real property owners. Property ownership in Russia made great strides after the start of capitalist development, but even the last emperor, Nicholas II, when answering a question about his occupation during the 1897 census (Russia's first), proudly proclaimed himself to be *Khozyayn zemli Russkoy*, which can be translated not only as the master of the Russian land, but also its owner.

What was, for Nicholas Romanov, a kind of poetic license, was reality for Joseph Stalin, who was known as a *Khozyayn* (Master) to his entourage. Stalin, who personally did not care for luxury, actually owned one-sixth of the world's surface and its more than 200 million inhabitants. The state was everything, and everything belonged to it. Personal property, such as cars (Soviet law did not recognize *private* property), was allowed, but strict limits were set on how much of it was permissible. Adding a second story to a shack which served as a family's country house, for example, was not. Even the high and mighty of the ruling party were only allowed to use, not own, their palatial dachas. The latter were taken away at the time of their dismissal, retirement, or death.

Russia's privatization, overseen by Anatoly Chubais, was the biggest in scale, and probably most widely criticized in history. Usually, the focus of accounts is on the rich and the super-rich and the grossly unfair and often criminal ways of enrichment. Personal histories of Berezovsky and Khodorkovsky have provided ample material for movie thrillers in the hallowed tradition of *The Godfather*. Others, focusing on generic types rather than individuals, such as *Brigada* (Brigade) or *Brat* (Buddy), have become post-Soviet classics. Still, Russia today boasts (if that's the correct way to put it) 33 billionaires (still 12 times fewer than in the United States and behind Germany, but ahead of the rest of the world). However, there is another side to the story.

In the Soviet Union, the most valuable piece of personal property was a car, costing 50 to 100 times the average monthly salary. Since the early 1990s, tens of millions of Russians have come to own their apartments, which they can rent, lease, or sell for real money. For some, it is very big money. In Moscow, as of this writing, apartments are priced at over $4,000 per square meter, and renting a small studio costs upwards of $500 per month. The property world does not stop at the front door of an apartment. Dachas outside big cities (many of them no longer resembling Soviet-era shacks) belong to millions; shares in publicly traded companies or mutual funds belong to hundreds of thousands. In 2006, Rosneft managed to attract 115,000 Russian buyers on the eve of its initial public offering (IPO). In 2007, the number one and number two banks, Sberbank and VTB, offered their own IPOs, with the Kremlin hoping to give a boost to Russia's people's capitalism. There is also a booming stock market, and popular mutual funds register a huge and rising inflow of cash.

Despite the much-publicized conflicts over property redistribution (the trials of Mikhail Khodorkovsky and Platon Lebedev and the seizure of Yugansk, the main producing unit of their YUKOS company), property relations are becoming routinized. Not in the sense of people's becoming less interested, just the opposite. Most of today's conflicts are about infringements of property rights at the grassroots level. People swindled by property developers demand justice across the country. Residents of city suburbs, from Moscow to Ufa, sue the local authorities for driving them off their land for inadequate compensation. Even detective stories, so popular among the Russian viewers and readers, now place the issue of property ownership at the center of their tales. Marrying into a rich family and inheriting a fortune have ceased to be just plots from nineteenth-century British and French novels. Russia's story after 1991 is that of very rough, brutal, and cheerful capitalism.

Private property equals freedom in a broad sense (to begin with, one becomes the "owner" of one's life) and in a more specific sense, with degrees of freedom proportional to the amount of property one owns. From the English barons of the Magna Carta era to the robber barons of Russia's "rocky nineties," freedom usually begins at the top and trickles down over time. That is why Khodorkovsky's fate was so important, and the situation of the moneyed elite remains so today. Their demise at the hands of the supreme authority is not good news for the common man. However, once people have become assured as property owners, the very nature of their relations with the state changes. The state can no longer simply confiscate the property of the government's opponents, and thus dispossess their families. It cannot move people around with ease. It cannot invade people's private lives in every sphere. Instead, the notion of privacy, for which translators until recently had no ready equivalent in Russian, is taking root. Indeed, at the beginning of the twenty-first century Russia, once a paragon of collectivism, has largely gone private. Individualism is spreading, often at the expense of solidarity. More and more people are interested in making a good living for themselves.

A Consumer Society

Of course, in this new situation it is impossible to talk about equality. One could generalize about the Soviet Union. Apart from the *nomenklatura* elite, most Soviet citizens lived in roughly similar and mostly squalid conditions. Critics of the Soviet system called this equality in misery. Russia, by contrast, is a highly unequal place.

At the top, there are about 3 percent who are wealthy people, and 7 percent who are doing well. Below them, some 20 percent can be described as the emerging middle class. At the bottom of the social pyramid, at least 20 percent are poor. There are huge disparities. The income of the top 10 percent is 15 times larger than the income of the bottom 10 percent. However, it is those in the middle of the societal structure, roughly 50 percent of the population, who are caught in transition. Most of them should be able to make it to the middle class group; should this happen, it would stabilize society enormously and seal Russia's success. However, if they were to sink into the poor underclass, Russia would find itself in dire straits. The stakes could not be higher.

So far, the arrival of private property has lifted most boats in this vast country. While officially Russia's Gross Domestic Product (GDP) has yet to catch up with the last Soviet-era high, virtually all Russians are considerably better off than ever before. Russia's 2006 per capita GDP (PPP) is above U.S. $13,000, comparable to that of Turkey, slightly lower than Poland, and considerably superior to Ukraine. In Moscow, at $20,000–$25,000, it stands at the level of Western European cities, far above central and eastern European capitals. The number of cars in

Moscow has reached 3 million, making the city of 10 million people virtually impassable at any time. As one approaches any Russian provincial center, one sees clusters of redbrick structures, modestly called cottages, and often costing hundreds of thousands or millions of dollars. To anyone who lived in the Soviet Union or even visited there, the current availability of various goods and services, often around the clock every day of the week, is truly astounding. One never forgets that the Soviet GDP consisted to a significant extent of defense-related production, rather than consumer goods.

Indeed, private consumption has become the principal driver of Russian economic growth. Citizens (in the elevated sense of members of a civil society) have not arrived in Russia yet, but consumers have. People are voting with their rubles, and the importance of the ruble vote is not to be underestimated. To better understand what's going on, one needs to place something like an "IKEA index" (named after the Swedish home furniture and appliance chain) next to the much better-known Freedom House table. At this writing, the number of IKEA stores stood at five, with eleven more in the works. At this juncture in their history, Russians, while apathetic toward politics, are avid consumers, aiming to improve their personal lives. This is a major development. On TV, the public demands around-the-clock entertainment rather than politics. The widening network of shopping malls across Russia is a symbol of the spread of the emerging middle classes.

Russia Does Not Live by Moscow Alone

These changes are not taking place solely in the capital or a handful of major cities. Each provincial center in the country is a little Moscow to its neighborhood. Living in Moscow has ceased to be what it was in Soviet days: the only way to have guaranteed access to more or less decent food, a relatively well-paying job, and entertainment. Russia has gone provincial and regional; it is "coming home." While politically under the Kremlin's tight control, economically, socially, and culturally, the cities and major towns are in the process of establishing themselves. Regional identities are emerging. The best way to gauge the pace of regional development is not to compare the individual regions to Moscow, but to themselves ten or twenty years ago.

One such example is Sergiev Posad, a city of 120,000 residents 50 miles northeast of Moscow. From the late 1970s until about 1994, every year was worse than the one before. Then, all of a sudden, things started to pick up. Retail trade expanded greatly; housing construction boomed; roads were repaired; the car population exploded; restaurants sprang up, some offering Japanese and other Asian food; and banking services became available. Five days after the official introduction of the Euro, the notes were available at a local exchange office. Similar stories could be told about hundreds of other places between Kaliningrad and Sakhalin.

The wealth trickles down and spreads across the country, highly unevenly. The story of emerging capitalism has many faces, all of which belong together and cannot be separated at will. Gross inequality has been mentioned. Corruption has reached historically unprecedented proportions in a country where official bribe-taking and stealing from public funds has been a problem for centuries. Economic crimes are part of the general lack of public safety. Pervasive materialism is destroying whatever values have survived the Soviet transformation.

Capitalism also has many opponents in the country, where personal wealth had never been regarded as rightful compensation for one's labor, but rather as a result of stealing, usually in collusion with the authorities, or as a favor from them. In few countries has property been so shallowly rooted as in Russia. The legal system, without whose independence and professionalism no private property can be safe, is not yet really in place. Political expediency, as in the YUKOS case, is undermining the fundamental principles about which the authorities appear agreed and which serve their own wider interests.

Russia's exercise in building capitalism is greatly facilitated by the advance of globalization and the *flattening of the world*, to use Thomas Friedman's concept. The good thing is that it is doing it under conditions of unprecedented openness to the outside world.

Openness to the Outside World
Next to money and private property, the driving force behind Russia's change is the country's physical openness. For three quarters of a century, Russia had been effectively isolated from the outside world. The Soviet border had become a true Iron Curtain decades before Winston Churchill coined the phrase in his 1946 speech in Fulton, Missouri. The USSR was self-contained, self-sufficient, and self-sustaining. The Russian Federation is exactly the opposite.

Communist ideology, which proclaimed class-based antagonism toward the West, became a victim of capitalist development, even before the official end of the Soviet Union. It is rather noteworthy and ironic that the current phase in Russia's capitalist evolution is so closely linked with former KGB officers. In the final decades of the Soviet Union, these were among the most nonideological, pragmatic, ruthless, often cynical, and, in their own way, highly individualistic people within the Soviet system. They refused to save the moribund system and were among the first to treat themselves to the new opportunities. It was the things that these former officers, including Vladimir Putin, learned in the freewheeling 1990s that made them what they are today.

Today, the closest thing to an ideology is official patriotism, propagated by those who made themselves rich and now crave recognition. This is anything but abstract or sentimental. The patriotism of the rulers stands for support and, if need be, defense of the status quo, which allows the elites to prosper, and for active competition with others in the international marketplace of economic products, political influence, military might, soft power attractiveness, and ideas.

Freedom of Worship

Freedom from ideology opened up society. Freedom of worship was the first right to become a reality. Since 1988, when the still officially communist state joined the Russian Orthodox Church (ROC) in celebrating the millennium of Christianity in Russia, the ROC has moved to occupy a central place in Russia's spiritual realm. In the same period, Muslim revival was no less conspicuous and even more vibrant. Judaism was officially recognized as an indigenous religion, and official antisemitism became history. Russian Buddhists were able to re-establish links with the Dalai Lama, who had made several trips to Russia before Moscow succumbed to Beijing's protests. The Bible, the Koran, and the Torah, as well as religious literature, virtually banned or severely restricted in Soviet times, are now widely published and freely distributed.

The situation is anything but idyllic. Though the Chechen war was generally free of religious overtones, rising xenophobia is targeting immigrants from the former Soviet South, many of them Muslim. Again, though the dismantlement of the oligarchical rule did not lead to a resumption of official antisemitism, a number of synagogues have been attacked. Also, in contrast to the four established religions, members of other Christian confessions, such as Catholics, Protestants, and Old Believers, though they have been able to function, are regarded as outsiders and operate under certain restrictions. The ROC's stand against Catholic "proselytism" in Russia and the proliferation of Protestant "sects" has influenced the Russian government's relations with the

Vatican and attitudes toward Western Christendom more generally. Still, the fact remains that Western Christians can and do expand their presence across Russia's borders.

Freedom of Movement

The Soviet Union was a walled-in society. Soviet citizens could not travel abroad, especially in the West, other than on government business or as part of government-approved delegations or groups. In a very few carefully selected cases, they were permitted to travel by themselves, subject to a later review of their behavior. They were not allowed to keep passports for foreign travel at home. But even if they did, that would not have meant much: before a Soviet citizen could buy a ticket and apply for a visa at a foreign embassy, one had to get an *exit visa* from the Soviet authorities. In the second half of the 1980s, when freedom of speech was already becoming a reality, but freedom of movement was still out of reach, a popular comedian set packed audiences roaring by a seemingly innocuous comment: "I need to go to Paris on urgent personal business!" When I tell this to my sons, born in the 1980s, but raised in the 1990s, they don't get the joke.

In 2005, 6.5 million Russians traveled abroad, with Turkey, China, and Egypt, all holiday destinations, topping the list. There are several dozen international airports, whereas Moscow was the sole port of entry and exit in Soviet days. Millions have used the new freedom and emigrated to the four corners of the globe. Three countries—Israel, Germany, and the United States—each have become home to over a million former Soviet nationals. About a million and a half, however, prefer to keep their Russian citizenship, even though they permanently reside abroad (over 300,000 in London alone). Whenever a disaster happens any-where abroad (a tsunami in the Indian Ocean, a hurricane in New Orleans, a plane crash anywhere in the world), Russian news media routinely mention whether there have been Russian casualties.

Freedom of Speech

As discussed above, the commanding heights of the media, i.e., television stations, are under the Kremlin's control. In general, one can freely discuss and criticize the government's policies privately or publicly, but the degree of freedom varies according to the medium. The printed press is still generally free. There has been some expansion of government-friendly ownership and a degree of self-censorship, but the latter is closer to Western-style conformity and political correctness than to the crude Soviet model. Boris Berezovsky, the archenemy of President Putin, owned two of Moscow's high-quality newspapers for years after he himself had emigrated. Radio has a few outlets of genuinely free speech, including the indomitable Echo Moskvy. Television, however, is largely state-controlled. It is more useful as a means of knowing what the authorities want the public to believe than a source of "news." Until recently, only REN-TV dared to be critical of the authorities after the forced closure of "old" NTV and TV-6, the two opposition stations. Ironically, the exiled former media mogul Vladimir Gusinski keeps a small station, RTVi, which broadcasts from Moscow to Russian-speaking audiences abroad.

The Internet, by contrast, is free, and has a growing number of lively and outspoken news sites. Foreign newspapers and magazines are on sale, mostly in Moscow, although their readership is small. The local circulation of the *International Herald Tribune*, which started printing in Moscow in 2006, is a mere 2,000. Satellite and cable TV are available in all major cities. Foreign news items and analyses that concern Russia, including the more critical ones, are picked up, translated, and posted on Russian-language web sites. There is big demand for Western glossy magazines specializing in fashion, style, health, sports, and entertainment. Many of them have started Russian editions.

Virtually all literature banned in Soviet times, a huge backlog of émigré and dissident authors, has been published. Western political books—some highly critical of Russia's past and present policies, including those by Zbigniew Brzezinski and Richard Pipes or by former Soviet spies who emigrated to the West, such as Victor Suvorov, Oleg Gordievsky, Vasily Mitrokhin, Oleg Kalugin, and Alexander Litvinenko—have been translated and appeared in Russia. The Russian book industry publishes a large number of political treatises of all persuasions, including memoirs by George H. W. Bush and Brent Scowcroft, Bill Clinton, Madeleine Albright, Colin Powell, and Strobe Talbott. But as with newspapers, the print runs are determined by the demand of the market.

A Changing Society

These monumental changes are quickly changing society. Perestroika, which started the present cycle of change in Russia, is now more than two decades old. Not only teenagers, but young people in their twenties have no firsthand experience with the Soviet Union. They are, in fact, Russia's first free generation. It is simplistic, of course, to expect the younger generation to automatically embrace democracy and other values of an advanced society. There are yuppies making lots of money, and there are young unemployeds from the industrial suburbs and former company towns. Most are patriotic and quite a few are chauvinistic. The latter, having never lived in the USSR, adore it as a great power that held much of the outside world in awe.

Of all things in Russia, societal values are undergoing perhaps the roughest transformation and the biggest distortions. It would be safe to say that, in today's Russia, material values clearly dominate. Ordinary Russians are less idealistic than ever before. Abstract ideas no longer produce selfless enthusiasm. Those who feel strong are individualistic and pursue happiness for themselves and their families as best they can. Those who feel weaker take the state to task for not being sufficiently protective of their interests. There are very few strikes. Most mass protests come from middle-class people who have been victimized by criminals. Everywhere, collectivist values and solidarity are in steep decline. There is no "system" of values that has replaced the communist one. Too much is still in flux, and many people are disoriented. However, what is slowly emerging is far from inimical to the value systems prevailing in America or Europe. In fact, the situation in which many Russians find themselves can be compared to the periods in the history of Western capitalism depicted by such authors as Charles Dickens and Theodore Dreiser or, closer to home, by the Russian writers of the late nineteenth century. The one major difference is that now the new order is succeeding Soviet urbanized socialism, not traditional agricultural society. The actual gap in values between contemporary Russia and the West is thus related to historical stages rather than ideologically inspired.

How to bridge that gap? Who can play the role of the system modernizer if Russian society does not agree to fully subcontract that task to the government, i.e., the Kremlin?

Whence the New Quantum Leap?
The state of affairs described above can only be transient, because there is too much disequilibrium. Russia is not yet over the hump, and things could go in any of many directions. Early successes in post-communist transformation should not lead to complacency. Czarist Russia was doing pretty well in 1913, only to stumble into a war the following year and perish in a revolution just three years after that. Corrupt and arrogant elites may yet bring about a surge in left-wing populism allied with right-wing nationalism to send Russia on the path to a new catastrophe. Three best-selling novels in 2006 painted a very bleak future of the country ten to twenty years from now: at war with itself, isolated from the outside world, and having nothing better to do

than to destroy itself. Yet Russia is certainly not doomed to follow those prophecies. There are protest forces pulling in a different direction.

Only recently, the most serious hopes were attached to Russian big business. The arrival under Yeltsin of the oligarchical regime allowed outside observers to say that even if Russia were not democratic five years after the fall of communism, it was at least demonstrably plural-ist. The idea was that, with the state forced to give up its deadly grip on power, the oligarchs would be able to agree on a political settlement based on market principles, limited government, regionalism, and individual freedoms. The transformation of the oligarchs themselves, in a Saul-to-Paul fashion, was seen as a vivid emblem of Russia's progress.

This was not to be. The deterrent effect of the Khodorkovsky case is hard to overestimate. By the early 2000s, big business had ceased to be a big player in Russian politics. Its representative chamber, the Russian Union of Industrialists and Entrepreneurs (RSPP), once vocal and seemingly powerful, is now a thoroughly loyal lobbying group devoid of any political ambitions. Even if one accepts that the old oligarchs have been succeeded by the new ones, who combine big money with positions of high authority, the notion of an "oligarchical way" to political pluralism and ultimately democracy in Russia should be discarded.

However, there is one area where the selfish interests of the oligarchs, especially the new bureaucratic tycoons, could play a constructive role. Since the ruling corporation has to rotate its leaders, some of whom are figureheads, to gain indispensable legitimacy from the citizens its members will be inherently interested in protection of their private property (and likely personal freedom as well) as a change at the Kremlin occurs. They will seek the legitimization of their ill-gotten wealth. One way to procure such a guarantee is to handpick a succes-sor and reach a deal with him before the succession. However, in such a case there are bound to be not only winners, but also important losers, whose interests will be at risk. With each new transfer of power, and with the incorporation of each new elite group into the corporation, the risks to the ruling elite as a whole will rise. Thus, institutionalizing private property rights eventually emerges as the preferred option for all. This can only be done by strengthening the legal system. Thus, the greed of the powerful few could eventually pave the way for the rule of law.

By contrast to corporate giants, medium-sized and small business plays a very modest role in Russia. Currently, they account for a puny 20 percent of the GDP. These businessmen suffer the most from bureaucratic corruption. However, unlike the high-flying tycoons, they cannot leave the country and take much of their capital with them. They will have to remain in Russia and either accept the ever-growing burden of the corruption tax, which could drive them out of business altogether, or start organizing to defend their interests. There is a chance that, a dozen years down the road if not earlier, they may start building coalitions for effective governance, which in practice would stand for cleaner and more accountable government at the level where they do business. In the first instance, this will not be a revolt against the Kremlin, no *lèse-majesté*. However, mayors, town councils, and regional legislatures will gradually become more responsive to the interests of local business communities and other special interests.

Mass political activity is likely to start as nonpolitical protests. The potential for that is already there. When the government decided in 2004 to do away with the vestiges of the Soviet welfare state (which was the right thing to do), but failed to properly implement the law that had just been enacted, a sudden a brush fire of street protests engulfed the country. Those worst hit (pensioners first of all) filled main squares and blocked main streets. There was no question of suppressing this wave of protest, or even of trying to hush it up. Protests were shown on TV, and the government appeared at a loss. The NGOs, previously dormant, found a cause. In the end, the government had to do what it should have done in the first place: explain its policies, persuade the public, and adjust the legislation. The principle of abolishing the system, which could and should no longer be supported, was honored. But society won an important battle. Interestingly, there has been no violence on either side.

Another example puts the spotlight on the budding self-consciousness of the emerging middle class. In the early 2000s, a party of car owners was formed, but it was seen as an oddity on par with the beer-lovers party, and had a very brief existence. However, when in 2005 a governor in the Altai region in southern Siberia was killed in a car accident (his limousine was traveling 125 mph on a narrow road with no escort) and the driver of a passing car was unfairly implicated and sentenced to prison, car owners across the country spontaneously organized rallies to send a message to the authorities. The protests were so wide-ranging that the party in power, United Russia, thought it wise to support them and help overturn the verdict. But the car owners' movement then adopted another cause: thousands of drivers across Russia tied white ribbons to their car antennas to protest against the privileges of "special vehicles" carrying government officials or their friends or relatives. The privileges are not going to be abolished, even significantly trimmed, but the message is worth noting. Since Soviet days, owning a car has been an outward symbol of affluence and a measure of freedom. Car owners *are* the middle class. They are paying taxes. Over time, they will insist not only on good roads, but good governance as well.

Other changes with a potential political import are likely to come from people's homes. Since the state has stopped subsidizing communal services and utility companies, residents will have to pay up—and can be expected to demand high-quality services in return. Typically, in today's Russia people's apartments are reasonably well kept. However, staircases are usually in much worse shape. The backyards are simply neglected. The elite, of course, live more comfortably, shielded behind high fences and guard posts, but they have to pay for exclusive services. But as more ordinary people become more affluent, they will start looking around them. To be able to get anything done, they will need to organize. Condominiums, still very rare in Russian cities, will probably become a basic form of self-government. Demanding accountability from those on the lowest rungs of authority will ultimately lead to the birth of communal politics.

That said, the critics who lay all the blame for the democracy deficit at the gates of the Kremlin are only half right. Certainly, Putin and his likely successors are not, and do not consider themselves to be, the champions of democracy. However, at the other end of the spectrum, there is still precious little *demand* for democracy. This does not mean that Russians are totally apathetic, passive, and submissive. Rather, it appears that their thoughts have turned from the sweeping slogans of the late 1980s to rather practical matters. But it is these same practical matters that will lead them back into politics, possibly through the back door.

The need to legitimize huge wealth at the very top; the business community's interest in stable and fair rules of the game; the middle class's pressure for good governance; and the pressure of the norms of the World Trade Organization, to which Russia aspires to accede, all point to either things in Russia continuing to change through a new round of reforms or to crises. Some crises would lead to breakthroughs; others may open the floodgates to a popular backlash against Russian capitalism with its glaring inequalities. Populism, which would come in nationalist and socialist garb, is the most serious potential threat facing Russia in the foreseeable future.

The liberalism of the intelligentsia in the form of pro-democracy and human rights movements has played a great and indispensable historical role. It helped undercut the Soviet communist system and offered a broad democratic alternative. However, in the twenty-first century, "intelligentsia liberalism" is a thing of the past. Its surviving venerable leaders are already respected historical figures, rather than still prime agents of change. This is a hard blow to the individuals concerned, most of whom are still young, physically fit, and intellectually vigorous. However, this should not be a cause for despair. New liberalism is likely to arise in a seemingly unlikely place, among the entrepreneurs who will need freedom to survive and the middle classes, who would form their political base. This will be a nation-building experience.

Russia, a Nation State

Post-Soviet Russia is in the midst of nation building, but of a different kind than her former borderlands. Since the mid-sixteenth century, Russia had been evolving as an empire. Count Sergei Witte, prime minister under Nicholas II, famously said that *there was no such thing as Russia, only the Russian empire.* It was an empire, however, that lacked a clearly defined metropolitan territory. The Soviet Union perished because a significant part of the Russian elite had decided to dump the borderlands. This was supported by the Russian population, who had grown weary of empire. The breakup of the USSR marked the end of the 500-year-old empire and the birth of a Russian nation state. However, creating a nation has turned out to be more difficult than accommodating to new (and in the opinion of many, unfairly drawn) borders.

In principle, a number of key building blocks are available. Ethnic Russians are numerically dominant in today's Russian Federation. Orthodox Christianity could emerge as a spiritual anchor. The imperial heritage would allow Russians to integrate others into their midst without much difficulty. When Boris Yeltsin first started addressing his fellow citizens as *rossiyane,* i.e., Russian nationals, as opposed to *russkie,* or ethnic Russians, it sounded strange and artificial. A decade and a half later, it is used with absolute ease and sounds perfectly natural. In principle, anyone can be a Russian (in the sense of a *rossiyanin*), provided he or she is prepared to Russify (learn to speak the language, share in the common heritage, and so on). Language proficiency, the use of a patronymic in the full name as an outward expression of integration into the community, and formal citizenship are the three basic features of a Russian. However, there are problems.

There are about 20 million ethnic Russians in the former borderlands, such as the Crimea, where they form a two-thirds majority, or in eastern and southern Ukraine, or northern Kazakhstan, who are not Russian citizens. However, the majority in the separatist enclaves of Abkhazia, South Ossetia, and Transnistria, which have been functioning as de facto states, have been recently awarded RF citizenship. While the project of dual citizenship between Russia and CIS countries, proposed by Moscow in the early 1990s, was a nonstarter in the eyes of the new states, Russia has come up with the vague category of "compatriots," which includes former Soviet citizens and descendants of Russian imperial subjects. This was done with an eye to the worsening demographics in the country.

The demographic question is often described as a crisis. Russia's population is declining at an annual rate of 700,000–800,000. Russia is no longer the fourth largest nation in the world, as the USSR was (behind China and India and close enough to the third-place United States). With 143 million inhabitants and falling, the Russian Federation has plunged to ninth place. Bangladesh and Pakistan have overtaken it. If current trends continue, Russia's population will drop to approximately 100 million by 2050—fewer people than Iran. "The demographic catastrophe has arrived!", "Russia is dying out!": these cries can be heard daily in the Russian media.

Yet, even 100 million in 2050 would be the equivalent of the 1950 population of the Russian Soviet republic. True, this was a count taken soon after the bloodiest of all wars, and after the preceding two decades of civil and border wars, revolutions, famine, collectivization, purges, and so on. However, population density is not the central issue. Most Russian territory, as in Canada, is not fit for permanent settlement and will remain so. As for the demographic balance with China, it never existed and cannot be established. If the entire Russian population were moved to the Russian Far East, that would only balance the combined population of just three Chinese provinces across the Amur and Ussuri rivers.

The real cause for concern is the wellness of Russia's population, not its size. Physical and mental health, education levels, professional skills, and living and working standards have all deteriorated since the end of the Soviet welfare state. Life expectancy, which had taken a plunge in the early 1990s, remains notoriously low (67.66 years, compared to Poland's 73), especially for males (just under 60). Between 500,000 and 700,000 people die of alcoholism or alcohol-related causes every year, and 35,000 die in road collisions. Twenty percent of youngsters use drugs, if occasionally. The number of street children, not all of whom are orphans, is over 700,000. Yet, things are not all gloom and doom. The upper strata of society are adopting habits of healthy living. In the major cities, sports clubs and fitness centers are mushrooming. The availability of high-quality medical care and medications has expanded to include most average income earners. Most strikingly, the nation's drinking habits are changing. Beer and wine have entered the territory of vodka.

Exiting from empire is never easy. After a period of shock and intense humiliation, national resurgence follows. In contrast to France and Britain, Russia's immediate post-imperial existence has not been accompanied and compensated for by integration into a larger entity such as the European Community and the Atlantic Alliance. The predictable result is a palpable rise in modern Russian nationalism. Most Russians have grown tired of pleading to be excused for the wrongs of the Soviet Union. They acknowledge the past, but are no longer willing to take the blame or repent. Conservative patriotism has become the hallmark of the Putin presidency.

Even as the Russian government tries to solve the looming problem of a labor deficit by stimulating immigration, new demons are rearing their heads. The demand for foreign labor has been matched by supply. Since the demise of the USSR, 6 million people have legally moved to Russia from the newly independent states. The number of illegal immigrants is estimated at about 10 million. This has provoked anti-immigrant violence, especially in the major cities. There have been no pogroms; it is mostly individual acts of violence. The anti-immigrant slogan "Russia for the Russians" receives broad support from public opinion. In a number of cases, jurors acquitted those charged with attacking Central Asian immigrants, African students, and Asians. This undermines Russia's nation-building effort as well as the unity of the Russian Federation.

To counter runaway nationalism, the Kremlin has traditionally relied on the support of Gennadi Zyuganov, head of the Communist Party, on the left and Vladimir Zhirinovsky, a rabid nationalist, on the right. The former de facto emasculated communism, including its internationalist class doctrine, and replaced it with a soft version of conservative, Orthodox Christian-inspired, and socially conscious nationalism. The latter attracted "hard-line" nationalists, sucked in by the pent-up dark energy of national humiliation, and neutralized it in thunderous pronouncements, scandalous talk shows, and extravagant, occasionally obscene clowning. As a result, for more than a decade would-be nationalist outbursts were treated by most observers as a tempest in a teapot, as ordered by the Kremlin. Now this is hardly sufficient. The Kremlin has obviously decided to disarm the nationalists by adopting and adapting some of their slogans. Toward the end of his second term, President Putin assumed the mantle of a moderate nationalist and protector of the "indigenous population."

Conclusion: Up or Down?

Despite many positive trends, Russia's future is by no means assured. A hundred years ago, it was also sailing in the right direction, only to sink shortly before its destination. This time, the potential for failure is still uncomfortably high. Although physical disintegration of the country is rather unlikely, a populist and nationalist backlash against the greedy and irresponsible elites is possible. A more probable "way down" would be led by runaway corruption, which would turn Russia into a huge petrostate, deepening downward dynamics in health, demographics, science and technology, and education, which would ensure that Russia became a backward periphery of both Europe and Asia, what the Russians call sarcastically "Aziopa," which could roughly (and irreverently) be rendered as *Ass-i-opa*.

The "way up" passes through a second (capitalist) modernization, which would replace the traditional model of extensive development with an intensive one. This requires institution building, starting with guaranteeing private property rights and establishing an independent judiciary, the rule of law, and constitutional government. It requires Russia's consolidation as a nation and its integration into the international community as a market economy and a modern polity.

Even though such a modernization process would take decades and probably generations, Russia has all it needs to finally make it. It is definitely not the Soviet Union. Modern Russian capitalism is real and growing. Expanding freedom, rather than ensuring full democracy, is the next big issue in Russian politics. Present-day Russia may bear some outward resemblance to the old czarist empire, and its task is to complete the journey to a functioning market economy, a strong civil society and representative and accountable government, which was cut short by the 1917 Bolshevik revolution.

A breakup of the Russian Federation is not in the cards. A world without Russia is a fantasy. It would be wrong to describe Russia's current state as decline simply by comparing its raw power and international influence with that of its Soviet predecessor. A more adequate description would be *reconstitution*, in which the very foundations of society are undergoing a change. How.does this Russia square with the world outside? The next chapter will look at the West, its beginnings, evolution, and prospects.

CHAPTER 2

WESTERN INTEGRATION
AND WESTERNIZATION

The end of the Soviet-led communist system abolished the "second world," a collection of communist-ruled states that challenged the "first world" of international capitalism. The former members of the group faced a stark choice: either climb to the "first world" of the West or plunge to the unenviable position of the least developed societies. East Germany became the first communist country to elect incorporation into the West, by means of simply merging into the Federal Republic of Germany, an option provided by the West German constitution. During the 1990s and the early 2000s, a number of central and eastern European countries have worked to fulfill the criteria of membership in the two premier institutions of the Western world, the North Atlantic Treaty Organization (NATO) and the European Union (EU). In 2007, the Atlantic Alliance (NATO) and the EU, which numbered 16 and 12 members, respectively, when the Berlin Wall fell in 1989, expanded to 26 and 27 countries, respectively.

While the degree of domestic transformation varies from country to country, all former members of the Warsaw Pact and its economic companion, CMEA or COMECON, and the three Baltic republics of the former Soviet Union, have passed the point where the changes became irreversible. For their elites and publics alike, "returning to Europe" and "joining the West" became more than political slogans or merely an elite exercise. These efforts captured historical yearnings and accomplished a generation's supreme national goals.

The ambitious vision of a free and united Europe is now a reality. The division of Germany and the wider Cold War divide have been overcome. NATO and the EU today include three Orthodox Christian countries and five mainly Slavic states. Neither organization's enlargement process is complete and more additions, mainly in the Balkans, are likely in the foreseeable future. The two enlargements, in effect, have erased the 1,000-year-old schism that separated western and eastern halves of Europe, led by Rome and Constantinople. With the ethnic, cultural, and religious features of its constituent parts intact, the continent has acquired a common political, economic, societal, and value-related infrastructure. From that perspective, virtually all Europe outside of the post-Soviet Commonwealth of Independent States (CIS) has fully joined the West. The question now is how far Europe will be willing and able to spread further from that common base.

The 2004 Orange Revolution in Ukraine and the 2003 Rose Revolution in Georgia offered a prospect for the triumph of Western ideas and principles all the way to the Russian border. The hope was that the progress in Ukraine would positively affect Belarus to the north and Moldova to the southwest, and that Georgia's success would turn the South Caucasus into a new Southeast Europe. Ukraine, Georgia, Moldova, and Azerbaijan transformed their loose association, GUAM, into a regional stability pact. The first three states are also members of the Community of Democratic Choice, alongside NATO/EU members, Poland and the Baltic states. Kiev and Tbilisi have also indicated their desire to join NATO and the European Union, although achievement of both goals by both countries in the foreseeable future is unlikely.

Internal developments in Ukraine and Georgia have so far failed to live up to initial expectations. The Orange coalition has broken down, and its opponent, defeated in 2004, emerged less than two years later as the powerful prime minister with a solid parliamentary majority. The Rose coalition is still holding, but popular resentment was growing until a deterioration of relations with Russia pushed the Georgians to rally around the flag. In terms of foreign relations, NATO's membership plan for Ukraine had to be shelved, and Georgia's intensified dialogue with the Alliance had to proceed against the background of heightened tensions around its two breakaway territories.

Yet, should the Ukrainian elites and the public agree about the packages of necessary reforms and move to implement them, with the support and assistance of Western countries, and if the Georgian government decides to make domestic development a priority, both countries can be transformed and eventually integrated into European and Euro–Atlantic institutions. As with central and eastern Europe, western integration would serve as a rising tide to help these countries modernize themselves faster and more fully.

Western integration can stretch over much territory and can be put to good use. In the Balkans, Croatia, Albania, and Macedonia, followed by Bosnia-Herzegovina, Montenegro, and finally Serbia and Kosovo would be able to "make it" to Europe. However, the ability of the West to integrate ever more countries has a limit, beyond which expansion turns into overextension. The different challenges can be illustrated by the dissimilar examples of Turkey and Russia.

Turkey has long been part of the Cold War West. It joined NATO in 1952 and applied for membership in the then-European Economic Community (EEC) in 1963. It made important and largely successful steps at modernization, first under Atatürk, and more recently, under successive civilian administrations from the 1980s onward. The problem with the Turkish EU bid is not so much Turkey, which, Muslim though it is, has gone a long way to meet Western standards and is prepared to continue moving ahead. Rather, the problem is Europe itself, which is unsure about the effects and implications of Turkish membership. By the time Turkey joins, it will count a population larger than that of Germany, making it the EU's largest member. Europe, especially since its failure in 2005 to ratify a European constitution, has entered another period of soul-searching over its future shape and structure, which puts both widening and deepening the union on hold.

While some may consider Turkey a borderline case, it may, indeed, be admitted, if Europe decides not only that it can absorb it, but that this gives the EU a totally different stature—and clout—in its Mediterranean and Middle Eastern neighborhoods. Again, the big question is whether Europe has the will to rise above being a highly successful, continental-size common market and assume a common political and strategic role that extends beyond its ever-changing borders.

The idea, popular in the 1990s, that Russia would be integrated as a full-fledged member the Western community inspired Russian democrats and their partners in Europe and America. Since the fall of the

Berlin Wall and the fall of communism in the Soviet Union, the idea of a Europe whole and free (and its variations: a common European home, a common space from Vancouver to Vladivostok, et al.) included fitting Russia into the West. Analogies were freely drawn with the post-World War II integration of West Germany and Japan (and, to make the same point from the opposite end, with Germany's treatment under the Versailles treaty and its consequences two decades later). Hopes were raised of a new Marshall Plan, early NATO membership, and some sort of a progressively tighter association with the EU.

Toward the end of the first decade of the twenty-first century, these hopes appear naïve pipedreams. Reality turned out differently, and why it did so will be analyzed in the next two chapters. What is important to discuss, at this point, is the phenomenon of the West itself. This notion is often used, but the meaning is not always the same, causing confusion and misunderstanding. Since the concept of Westernization is central to this study, the author will explain his view of the changing nature of the West and what this implies for Russia, which finds itself beyond the reach of Western institutions and, frankly, is not attracted by the idea of integrating into a larger unit.

Europe and the West

As noted earlier, European civilization has two main pillars, which are broadly associated with western and eastern Christianity. As a civilization, Europe extends from its geographical core all the way to North and South America to the west and to Siberia and the Russian Pacific coast to the east. It also covers Australia, New Zealand, and Israel. This huge area of a "global Europe" includes a multitude of cultures, but a single civilization, built on the common heritage of Christianity and Judaism and the ancient civilizations of Greece and Rome.

Russia as a whole belongs to this European civilization, although, like Latin America, it is off-center. The geographic border between Europe and Asia, which runs along the Ural Mountains, is absolutely irrelevant as a barrier to civilization. Russia, in fact, is easternmost Europe, not east of Europe. There is no point in drawing any kind of border along the Urals: Russia's provinces along the Pacific coast are the extension of eastern Europe, not of East Asia.

Part of the confusion originates in the fact that when the notion of Europe entered the political lexicon sometime in the seventeenth century, it succeeded the previous notion of the Occident, i.e., western Christianity. This narrow view of Europe, which for a long time saw its eastern border run from Königsberg to Kraków to Vienna, expanded over time. Today, in view of the actual and potential enlargement of the European Union, the narrow "Occidental" view has no real foundation whatsoever.

The concept of the West is different from that of Europe. Although it, too, has a geographical dimension, it is not linked to a particular civilization, but rather to a set of institutions, norms, and ideas that originated within European civilization in some of the countries of the old Occident. These institutions include private property; personal freedoms; the rule of law; constitutional and limited government; democratic participation; government accountability; and, most recently, human rights. These "best practices" were responsible for allowing the societies that embraced them to develop successfully, while guaranteeing their members freedoms and enabling them to achieve a degree of well-being.

Of course, the set of these "best practices" has been evolving. What was best in the sixteenth century was not good enough for the eighteenth, not to speak of the twenty-first. Between 1900 and 2000, the West has changed enormously. Authoritarian and totalitarian rule, however halting the process may be, were defeated, and colonialism, sexual discrimination, and racial segregation were rejected. However, the core principles remained and were expanded and built upon. This process is open-ended: the notion of the West has an ever-changing, self-improving content.

The march of the West is linked historically to the expansion of capitalism. Its birthplace is England and the Low Countries. In the sixteenth and seventeenth centuries they established the principles of private property rights, personal freedom, and representative government. In the eighteenth century, the United States of America, which had been Western even before it won independence, added the democratic principles of federalism and separation of powers with an independent judiciary. During the nineteenth century, France, Switzerland, and the Scandinavian countries further expanded the reach of the West. In the twentieth century, what distinguished the Western countries from capitalist non-Western ones were the principles of democracy and human rights.

The Impact of the World Wars
World War I saw a struggle between parliamentarian Britain and republican France, joined later by the democratic United States, all aligned with czarist Russia and authoritarian Italy and Japan against the

autocratic though law-governed Germany and Austria-Hungary, joined by the autocratic Ottoman Empire and Bulgaria. Though the allied group known as the Entente started as a classical geopolitical balance-of-power construct, it later acquired, mainly under the influence of President Woodrow Wilson, a broadly democratic character. The Allied war aims and Wilson's Fourteen Points were an early expression of emerging Western values in international politics, with their strong emphasis on national self-determination. In time, the Treaty of Versailles, founded on traditional principles of power relations, was accompanied by the Covenant of the League of Nations, which promised a better world. In addition, altruism started to become, as Henry Kissinger has observed, a steady drumbeat of American foreign policy.

These values, however, were operationally useless when the countries concerned failed to introduce Western institutions domestically. The salient result of World War I was the fall of authoritarian, monarchical regimes across Europe and the adoption of democratic constitutions, most notably in Germany and Austria. Democratization was also on the march in the victorious Western countries, notably in women's gaining the right to vote in Britain and the United States and in the institution of direct elections of members of the U.S. Senate.

It was in the interwar period that the perils of nondemocratic capitalist development became obvious. Germany failed to consolidate its fledgling democracy and succumbed to the temptation of National Socialism. Even earlier, Italy had developed a fascist corporate state. Authoritarianism spread to a number of countries across Europe, from the Baltic states and Poland to Austria and the Balkans to Portugal and Spain. Czechoslovakia was the only democratic exception in an increasingly authoritarian environment. Not all leaders were as aggressive or megalomaniac as Hitler and Mussolini, but virtually all shared in the ideology and practice of authoritarian control.

Like its predecessor, World War II did not begin as a clear-cut struggle between democracy and authoritarianism. Britain and France entered the war to defend quasi-authoritarian Poland after they had practically delivered democratic Czechoslovakia to Hitler. Geopolitical and strategic considerations carried the day.

The early democratic West was, to put it brutally, a miscarriage. Democracy, although it did receive a major boost after World War I, was still closely circumscribed. Women were granted the right to vote, and social democrats were entrusted with running governments, but class distinctions, not only in Eastern and Central, but also in Western Europe, still mattered greatly, making a number of countries vulnerable to domestic communist activities. A number of Western democracies possessed colonial empires, and often dealt harshly and wholly undemocratically with those seeking independence.

The West was also divided. The United States opted out of the League of Nations before it was constituted. The League itself was a talking shop, leaderless, and soon discredited by the squabbles among the major powers. Britain and France, allies in wartime, went separate ways once peace was achieved. Tragically, Germany was allowed in only grudgingly and belatedly. The world economic crisis of 1929–1932 undermined the feeble construction of its Weimar Constitution. When Hitler came to power, Germany still bore the stigma of war guilt and reparations.

It was the Second World War, however, that first produced a united democratic West. In 1940, Britain and France tragically embraced each other at the eleventh hour and vowed to merge their two states, but by that time France had been lost, and Britain was teetering on the brink of an abyss. It was Hitler's attack on the Soviet Union and his declaration of war on the United States, following the attack by Germany's ally Japan, that radically reversed the balance of forces against Nazi Germany.

To defeat a totalitarian power, one had to mobilize a superior military force, but to rehabilitate that nation, one needed an attractive democratic alternative. Britain's wartime alliance with the United States marked a new departure. The alliance was based on the 1941 Atlantic Charter, which became the first *common* manifesto of the democratic West. The exiled legitimate governments of the occupied nations of western and northern Europe, which joined the United States, Great Britain, and the latter's dominions, formed the core of what would become, for the first time, a lasting Western alliance.

That this alliance from the start had Anglo-American co-leadership at its core was exceedingly important. Not only did Anglo-Saxon unity provide for a high degree of cohesion, but the political-military coalition was based on a centuries-long heritage of the sanctity of private property, primacy of individual rights and freedoms, constitutional government, and well-developed legal systems. The war became an exercise in advancing democracy and freedom as much as in defeating the Axis' military might. Once the war ended, this became the principal task of the allies in the defeated and now-occupied former enemy countries.

The Soviet Union, which cooperated with the Western allies while it bore the brunt of the war in Europe, could not have been America's and Britain's soulmate on these issues. Stalin and his cohorts were sworn enemies of liberal democracy. Nazism, although it represented a major threat to the USSR, was much closer to Soviet communism in its origins and methods. From all that we know today, a version of the Cold War was natural and inevitable after World War II on both ideological and geopolitical grounds. Stalin was not a revolutionary firebrand; he was preoccupied with territorial arrangements, buffer zones, and spheres of influence abroad. However, even as the prestige of the Soviet Union and the Red Army was at its zenith, he clearly saw the danger to the system he had built at home from uncontrolled exposure to Western affluence *and* democracy. For Stalin, ideology was primarily a weapon of control. This was the ultimate Iron Curtain.

The Cold War: The West as We *Used to* Know It
When Europe became divided between the Western allies and the Soviet Union after the war, the West made only weak attempts at political integration. The U.S. expeditionary forces left Europe within three years. The new western union, grouped around Britain and France, was too loose and its leadership too weak. Germany lay prostrate, occupied, and partitioned. It took a Soviet challenge and an American response, a Truman with his "wise men" *and* a Stalin, his improbable counterpart, to produce what came to be known, for the next half-century, as *the* West.

Without the Prague coup and the Berlin blockade there wouldn't be a NATO; without the Korean War, NATO would not have an integrated military organization. By the same token, without a Marshall Plan, European economies would not have recovered so quickly and would have long remained under threat from local communist parties. West Europeans' own efforts at forging a "Europe," from a coal and steel community to an ill-fated defense organization and European army to, finally, the Treaty of Rome, were immensely important steps whose true significance was revealed only when the Cold War ended.

Meanwhile, the immediate need was to integrate the defeated enemies, West Germany and Japan, turned now into front-line states. This integration was accomplished by, first, their inclusion in peacetime military alliances led by the United States and, second, by Westernization, under close U.S. guidance, of their politics, and finally, by opening up their economies (admittedly, with more success in West Germany's case). It was then that Germany, previously thought of as the essential Central European country, re-identified itself as fully and exclusively Western, and Japan self-selected itself out of Asia and identified itself with the West. Both countries' sovereignty was limited, but this differed in degree, not in kind, from other U.S. junior allies' position during the Cold War.

In Europe, NATO became the principal instrument of integration, West Germany and Italy being its major success stories. The need to shore up the flanks led to the admission into the Alliance of Greece and Turkey. Outside of Europe, this function was performed by a system of bi- or trilateral alliances linking key regional countries, such as Japan, South Korea, Taiwan, Australia, and New Zealand to the United States, as well as looser and far less cohesive multilateral arrangements, such as the Southeast Asia Treaty Organization (SEATO), the Central Treaty Organization (CENTO), and the Rio Pact. Anticommunism was a must; military alliance a necessity; democracy, although obviously desirable, was neither.

In the 1950s and 1960s, NATO included dictatorships and military governments (such as in Portugal, Greece, and Turkey), with Franco's Spain a close collaborator, while several genuinely democratic countries—Sweden, Finland, Austria, Switzerland, and Ireland—were officially neutral. Meanwhile, the world's biggest democracy, India, was tilting, strategically, to the Soviet Union, and a communist country, Yugoslavia, was tilting *away* from it. Thus, outside of the hard core of North America, Western Europe, Japan, and Australia, grouped since 1960 in the Organisation for Economic Co-operation and Development (OECD), the "free world" consisted of pro-Western rather than Western states.

In retrospect, the late 1960s appear as a major turning point in the West's ongoing democratization. In different ways, America, France, and Germany went through national crises that affected their political cultures. In the 1970s, European economic integration both widened and intensified. The European Economic Community (EEC) was moving beyond the original common market. Institutional issues came to the fore in southern Europe and the Mediterranean. Greece, Portugal, and Spain began transitioning from military and police dictatorships to democracies. This transition, closely linked to integration with and into the EEC, was labeled "Europeanization." Turkey followed suit a few years later. In East Asia, rapid economic development in South Korea, Singapore, and Taiwan paved the way to modernization of their institutions.

The 1980s marked breakthroughs on several fronts. The EEC countries signed the Single European Act and moved in the direction of a political as well as economic union. A number of Asian countries, including South Korea, Taiwan, and the Philippines, edged toward political democracy. Deng Xiaoping opened China's doors to the outside world. In Latin America, military dictatorships collapsed throughout the region, succeeded by elected civilian governments. All this culminated toward the end of the decade in the fall of communism in Eastern Europe and the Soviet Union and the end of the Cold War.

The Post-Cold War West?

In the 1970s, the Soviet Union's chief America-watcher, Georgi Arbatov, liked telling his U.S. interlocutors: "We'll do something terrible to you; we'll deprive you of the enemy." The collapse of the Moscow-led "world socialist system" and the unraveling of the far-flung empire of Soviet client states, followed almost immediately by the breakup of the USSR itself and the dissolution of its Communist Party, remain unparalleled historical events both in scale and depth and in the relative smooth-ness, even civility, of nearly all the key events. They amounted to a self-annihilation of the most serious challenge to the Western system, which many once regarded as a credible alternative.

With the challenge gone, and the East no more, all of a sudden the West was standing tall, and alone. In this sense, it *was* the end of *a* history, the history of full-scale challenges to market democracy within "global Europe." It needs to be remembered that both the U.S.-led West and the Soviet-dominated East were two parts of the same civilization. Like the two world wars, the Cold War was essentially fought within European civilization and over ideologies that were products of the Enlightenment. The victorious West's first instinct was to stick together, because even though there was now no longer an identifiable enemy and the outside pressure had dramatically dropped, uncertainties about the future were immense.

The EEC, by means of the Amsterdam and Maastricht treaties, trans-formed itself into a European Union, abolishing most internal borders and sharing a common currency. The United States joined with Canada and Mexico to form a North American free trade area. By contrast, NATO fared much worse, coming closest to fulfilling Arbatov's prophecy, but it, too, kept itself in business by a combination of reaching out to former-adversaries-turned-partners, peace operations, and an air war against Serbia over the Kosovo issue.

Europe, no longer a ward of the United States, started to come into its own. The European Union offered an alternative model of the West: a network rather than a super-state. The EU prides itself on being communitarian rather than ruggedly individualistic. It has managed to achieve a high quality of life for most of its citizens. In fact, Europe itself has become a way of life, and a very attractive one at that. The outside world appreciates its soft power, in contrast to America's military might. In spite of all this spectacular progress, however, Europe has remained incoherent and indecisive on a number of crucial issues from adopting its own constitution to dealing with the Balkan wars in Croatia and Bosnia-Herzegovina. When Europeans finally acted, as later in Kosovo, they did so as part of NATO, thus following U.S. leadership.

What was particularly striking in the aftermath of the Cold War was the absence of a credible challenge from beyond European civilization. China, nominally communist, but nationalist in practice, did not care to pick up the mantle dropped by the Soviet Union. Instead, having repressed a pro-democracy movement at home in the name of preventing "great disorder under heaven," China intensified its market-oriented reforms. Democratic India embraced the market, started to walk away from statist policies, and warmed up to the United States. South Africa managed a transition from apartheid to majority democratic rule with its capitalist economy basically intact. An upsurge in globalization made the world move not only faster, but closer and in the same direction.

Was there a West at all now that "the Other" was gone? Some doubted it. To others, there was the West, integrating and expanding, and the Rest, recoiling but fractious and disorganized. Within two decades of the Cold War's end, the vast majority of former communist states of Central and Eastern Europe acceded to NATO and the European Union. Most of the "lands between" the expanded Euro–Atlantic community and Russia aspire to do the same, waiting only to meet the membership criteria and the opportune moment for entry. The conditions attached to the memberships ensured that the process of integration into NATO and especially the EU was a kind of a socio-economic-political tide which allowed aspiring nations to Westernize and EU-ropeanize faster.

The emergence at the turn of the twenty-first century of international terrorism, later referred to by President George W. Bush and others as

"Islamofascism," presented a serious threat to international security and a major political challenge to the West. These, however, were very different from the ones that the West had seen before. First, they came not only from another civilization (as had happened before with Japan), but from a singularly asymmetrical source: a network rather than a state. Second, the challenge was not universal and total, aiming to change the way of life in Western societies, and to take over Western states. Rather, its goal was to expel Western influence, particularly the U.S. military presence, from the Islamic world (and win concessions for its adherents elsewhere). Third, the inherent fractiousness of the Muslim world, with its Sunni vs. Shia, Persian vs. Arab divides, prevented consolidation of the hostile forces and allowed the West to contain the threat and take the battle to the enemy.

America's principal failure in that struggle was caused by its early decision to promote the right goals with inappropriate means. Islamist extremism had been a reaction to the challenges of globalization, which exposed the many vulnerabilities and inadequacies of Muslim, especially Arab, societies. The central front against the extremists lay clearly in the realm of politics, economics, and social life. Substitution of the individual for the collective lies at the very core of modernization. One needs to address the numerous injustices, inequalities, and lack of opportunities that accompany this transition. The challenge of extremism has to be countered by strengthening the forces of domestic modernization, by helping the Arab countries to integrate into the global economy and to identify and learn to exploit their comparative advantages.

The problem was that while these principles were put to work in a number of countries, from Morocco to Qatar and from Jordan to Kuwait, doctrinaire democracy promotion in Iraq made the United States miss the real opportunities for slower-motion nation (re)building and threatened to put into question its whole approach to the region. U.S. support for "revolutionary democracy" in Lebanon was countered by the rise of Hizbollah, and the introduction, with U.S. consent, of electoral democracy in the Palestinian territories produced a government led by Hamas. Finally, celebrating elections in a tribal, clan-ruled society as a major success of democracy, as in Afghanistan, could lead to wishful thinking. In a word, adopting ideology, a traditional instrument of control in totalitarian societies, as a guiding force of Western policy distorts the picture and robs the West of its comparative advantages. Had the United States tried to turn anticommunism into an ideology in the full sense of the word, the Cold War would have lasted longer and may have ended differently.

A better way to assist the modernization of the Middle East and help the forces of moderation prevail over their extremist opponents would include: disaggregating democracy into identifiable elements, such as governance and representation; proceeding step by step to promote the key elements of Westernism under the specific conditions of the Middle East, using the rich experience of Turkey and taking account of the Iranian experiment; focusing on improving education, providing health care, and creating jobs; and, finally, supporting moderate nationalism as a tool of nation building, while fostering regional contacts and compacts. Such a policy would pull the rug out from under those preparing for a clash of civilizations.

The antiterrorist coalition that emerged soon after September 11, 2001, offered the United States global leadership with the consent of virtually all nations, including Russia, China, and India. True, this was a very loose coalition, especially by comparison with the Cold War days of NATO. There should have been no illusion as to the diversity of the national interests of the countries involved. Most joined on the strength of those interests, rather than out of fealty to the United States. To lead such a coalition would have required a massive, brilliant, and nuanced effort, which would in part have gone unrewarded. Yet, the Bush administration never really tried that approach. It preferred to act alone, assisted by a coalition of the willing, i.e., its closest allies, such as Britain and Australia, or countries professing strong allegiance to the United States, such as Poland and Ukraine.

In time, the United States has managed to largely repair transatlantic relations. Yet, these relations will not return to the tightly knit Cold War alliance and will probably not be able to advance to a more equitable model of a U.S.-EU co-leadership. The very fact that European integration is not evolving toward a federal state imposes a limit on the EU as a hard-power actor and as a symmetrical partner of the United States. Strategically, for the foreseeable future, the United States will continue to deal with the EU as largely an economic unit and with the individual European nation states on policy matters, while using NATO as a toolbox for tackling specific security issues.

Historically confined to the Euro–Atlantic area, NATO has recently ranged abroad and engaged in a mission in Afghanistan. Some want to turn the alliance into a global organization by opening it to countries in the Pacific, such as Japan, Australia, South Korea, and New Zealand. Others advocate Israel's entry as a way to finally resolve the Palestinian issue. All countries mentioned are not only long-time U.S. allies, but thoroughly Western in their domestic institutions and the values they espouse. Still, it is not very likely that a global NATO will emerge or, even if it does, that its value added will be significant.

An alternative would be to build a global community that united all of the world's democratically governed countries. The concept of a "Democratic International," alas, is inherently flawed. Outside of a fairly narrow circle of countries, smaller even than the OECD's current 30-nation membership, evaluation of democratic credentials would often be arbitrary and politically driven. A holier-than-thou exclusivity would inevitably create resentment, and even a mini-United Nations would retain some of the undesirable characteristics of its predecessor. With values no longer at issue, countries would focus on their national interests. How harmonious, however, are the interests of the United States, France, Brazil, India, South Africa, and Japan, to name but a few?

It is instructive also to look at the record in the aftermath of the "color revolutions" hailed as the harbingers of a democratic future in some of the most difficult regions of the world. The first such revolution, which in 2000 overthrew Slobodan Milosevic's regime in Serbia, did little to mitigate Serbian nationalism, make Belgrade an eager partner of the EU, or to push democracy-building in the country. The 2003 uprising in Georgia, which toppled Eduard Shevardnadze's generally pro-Western but weak and ineffective government, installed in power a group of Western-oriented politicians who routinely resort to time-tested local methods to control the country. The 2004 "revolt of the middle classes" in Ukraine did bring real pluralism and genuine elements of democracy to the second-largest former Soviet republic. However, pluralism has ensured that pro-Western forces are effectively balanced by those who want to chart a middle course between the European Union and Russia. Finally, the 2005 "Tulip Revolution" in Kyrgyzstan has resulted in an increase of power of the regional clans at the expense of the central authority, putting the unity of the new state in question.

This does not mean that all those events did not bring anything positive: they did. Each revolution was an important milestone, and each materially promoted the process of modernization in a post-communist society. What is to be discouraged is the propensity to look at them as markers putting countries in a certain category in the binary democratic vs. authoritarian worldview. This reminds one of how Soviet ideologues came up with various definitions that they applied to Moscow's allies in its struggle for influence in the Third World: "progressive," "socialist-oriented," and "revolutionary democratic" (which sounds rather current).

This ideological verbiage contributed to the misjudgment behind the Soviet Union's biggest politico-military debacle, its 1979 intervention in Afghanistan and the ten-year war that followed.

It would make more sense to bank on the spread of capitalism, which is a *sine qua non* for democratic development, and focus on global governance rather than democracy promotion. In the post-Cold War world, the West has ceased to be a geographically defined concept. The liberal and democratic order may have many local opponents among the world's authoritarians (although it has no global challenger). Capitalism, however, has virtually no sworn enemies. Anti- or alterglobalists want some kind of "globalization with a human face," but few are genuine anti-capitalists. Communist China and Vietnam, authoritarian Russia and Kazakhstan, democratic India and Brazil, majority-rule South Africa, and many others are emerging not only as new markets but as capitalist societies.

After the EU's "big bang" enlargement in 2004, followed in 2007 by the inclusion of Romania and Bulgaria, the EU has taken a break. Europe needs time both to integrate the new members and to overcome internal differences that prevented it from ratifying its first-ever Constitution. Further enlargement will be more difficult. Croatia might get in, followed by Albania, Macedonia, Bosnia-Herzegovina, Montenegro, and eventually, perhaps, Serbia and Kosovo. Turkey, an EU aspirant since 1963, faces growing uncertainty with regard to its chances of being invited to join, and the domestic support for European integration has been eroded. Ukraine, another long-shot EU hopeful, has been told not to bother for the next twenty years or so. Moldovans' best chance to join Europe in the foreseeable future is by procuring Romanian passports, not through their own country's accession. For several years, Georgia has been flying EU flags next to its own on ministry buildings in Tbilisi, but its road to Brussels will be very long. Neighboring Azerbaijan and Armenia face at least as many hurdles. Finally, in theory at least, Belarus, too, might be able to exercise its European option, but not before Alexander Lukashenko, "Europe's last dictator," leaves the scene. To sum up: while about a dozen countries on the EU's eastern periphery seek to join the Union, thus making Europe complete, only a few of them will be allowed in during the next decade. The others will form the EU's zone of attraction, which even now stretches all the way to the borders of Russia.

The EU's eastern dimension is paralleled by its Mediterranean one. Europe's zone of attraction includes the countries of the Maghreb:

Morocco, Algeria, and Tunisia. Just a couple of hundred miles from the EU's new member Cyprus lies Lebanon, a foothold of European influence in the Middle East. Israel, of course, has long been a Western enclave in the region. But Egypt and Jordan also feel Europe's proximity and are attracted by it. Further afield, the African Union (AU) is taking after the EU as an institution. When the rule of law becomes firmly established and leads to functioning democracy in sub-Saharan Africa, Europe will probably exercise even more influence across the continent where English, French, and Portuguese are freely spoken.

Looking east, Kazakhstan, the quintessential Eurasian state, is making rapid economic progress. True, its politics are broadly authoritarian, similar to Russia's. Yet, it looks increasingly capitalistic. Its newly confident leadership made a bid for the presidency of the OSCE in 2009. The United States and the EU need to support this flagship of regional modernization, giving it the coveted presidency, while insisting that Kazakhstan live up to the norms of the body it prepares to chair. A vibrant, successful Kazakhstan would be very good news both for its fellow countries of Central Asia and its big neighbors, Russia and China.

Shanghai's Pu Dong outshines its majestic Bund, even as Shanghai itself outpaces Hong Kong. But there are more fundamental changes. Mainland China is going Taiwanese in its economic and social dimensions, even as Taiwan itself integrates with the mainland economically. The heirs of Mao Zedong are avidly learning from the heirs of Chiang Kai-shek, and the CPC is a new Kuomintang. They are also learning from South Korea, which, like Taiwan, has managed a smooth transition from authoritarian to democratic rule.

China's embrace of capitalism changes the global equation and holds out the prospect of a world built on common business principles and eventually on a modicum of universally accepted values. The fast growth of the Indian and Brazilian economies, which have emerged, respectively, from the slumber of Fabian socialism and military rule, is making the case irresistible. In the twenty-first century, the old West of Europe and North America will not face the angry Rest of the World. It may find an ally in what could be termed the new West of countries breaking out to capitalism. These include some of the world's most populous, economically significant, resource-rich, and politically influential countries. This is great news for the world.

Conclusion

The expansion of traditional Western institutions, such as NATO and the EU, although not yet complete, is already reaching its limits. A global NATO is not in the cards, nor is the European Union emerging as a global strategic actor. A "democratic United Nations," even if possible, would be impractical. Meanwhile, the Euro–Atlantic West, a community of similarly organized and like-minded countries, which gradually emerged in the twentieth century, has now reached the limits of growth and the peak of its global influence.

Westernization, meanwhile, is spreading alongside globalization. Countries like China and India realize that they will be successful only to the degree that they are able to master modern institution building. As they "build capitalism," former communist and Third World countries are establishing institutions, such as secure property rights, the rule of law, and government accountability, which lie at the foundation of all Western economies, societies, and polities. Thus, a New West is emerging, composed of Asian, Latin American, eastern European, and African nations. This is very good news for the international community at the start of the twenty-first century.

Of course, there is nothing totally new about this phenomenon. Originally Protestant in culture, the West spread to Catholic, Orthodox, and even Muslim Europe. In the late nineteenth century, Japan embarked on a policy of Westernization, but in a way that allowed it to preserve its unique culture. In the early twentieth century, a similar feat was performed by Atatürk's Turkey. What is new is rather the scale and speed of the current development, which is global and very fast-moving.

Ironically, the New West sometimes looks and acts like the Old West, 40 to 400 years ago. The parallels roughly correspond to the per capita GDP levels (in purchasing power parity terms) of the "new" and "old" Westerners. For instance, Russia's 2000 corresponded to Italy's 1959, West Germany's 1953, and America's 1935. These comparisons, of course, are largely illustrative, but they help underscore an important point. Keeping these time gaps in mind can throw light on the domestic and foreign policy behavior of countries. It also provides insight into the prospect that values will evolve. The values gap is a real phenomenon, but it is neither ideological nor political; it is historical, and can be narrowed or closed as a result of societal development. Under the circumstances, globalization can be a vehicle of vertical mobility in the international system.

The values discussed above expressed in the essentially political institutions such as property rights and the rule of law should not be confused, of course, with values peculiar to a certain civilization, a group within it, or an individual nation. The role of religion in society, or of the government in the economy, and the attitude to capital punishment are some examples. Japan's accession to, and admittance into, the West is a useful model here.

Democracy, historically, is a fairly late child of capitalism. It is usually preceded by a period of liberal and constitutional development. There are few shortcuts here, but the process itself, driven by interests, is by and large reliable. That is not to say it carries no dangers. Both World Wars were fought by fairly advanced capitalist societies. Nazism and, more broadly, fascism were aberrations in otherwise "normal" development of major European countries. These risks should be dealt with. One way to prevent them is through a dedicated policy of integrating the New West with the old one.

From this perspective, Russia's example is doubly interesting. On the one hand, one deals with an important country, which remains a challenge to America and Europe both when it becomes weak and when it grows strong. On the other, many of the "lessons" of the West's Russia policy (and of Russia's policies toward the West) are generic and should be factored in when Americans and Europeans map out their strategies vis-à-vis China or Iran. The next two chapters will seek to distill those lessons.

CHAPTER 3

RUSSIA AND THE WEST

A country's identity is akin to human personality. It changes over time and yet preserves an essential continuum. Throughout its history, Russia's identity has been constantly changing, often radically so. This journey is not over, and vastly different options are open. Many factors, internal and external, have contributed to the making, remaking, and occasionally unmaking of Russia. Of these, Russia's attitude toward the West (and vice versa) often determined the country's view of itself and its role and mission in the world.

This chapter will first discuss the different historical personae of Russia, and their attitudes toward the West; it will then consider the roots and effects of Moscow's spectacular foreign policy revolution under Mikhail Gorbachev. Finally, it will seek to analyze the lessons learned by Russia's post-Soviet leadership under Yeltsin and Putin from their engagement with the West and how this has affected the country's current foreign policy and its potential evolution. What follows is not an attempt to recount more than one thousand years of Russian history in a few thousand words. The focus will be on Russia's identity and the historical patterns of its relations with the West.

From the perspective of Russian-Western relations, several key elements stand out. The defining one is Christianity. Russia had *its* Rome—Constantinople, "the second Rome," which in the early Middle Ages eclipsed the original one. Constantinople was the most powerful economic, political, and cultural magnet for the early eastern Slavs, later a model for Russia's political system and state-church relations, and, finally, a prime objective of Russian foreign policy.

The adoption of Christianity by Prince Vladimir of Kiev sealed the orientation of Rus and its successors to eastern civilization. The act of baptism occurred in 988, almost 70 years before the schism between the Catholic pope and the patriarch of Constantinople. When the split came, Rus naturally stayed within the Byzantine sphere, but still within Christendom. Thus, long before it emerged as a distinct entity, Russia's identification had been with eastern Orthodoxy. Its alphabet is based on the Greek one. It was of the East all right, but also of the broader West. Russia, in fact, is *very old* Europe.

Kievan Rus, of course, was a forerunner of three eastern Slav nations: Ukraine, Belarus, and Russia. The Grand Duchy of Moscow was the first historical personality of the Russian people. Its position vis-à-vis the rest of Europe was defined by several factors. Like the rest of the Occident, it was Christian, but it was Orthodox rather than Catholic. After Byzantium's demise at the hands of the Ottoman Turks (1453), Muscovy remained the only independent Orthodox Christian state in the world; after the incorporation of the Ukrainian and Belarusian lands into the Polish-Lithuanian monarchy, it was the only part of the former Rus that governed itself. It was the easternmost Christian kingdom in Europe, a frontier state, vulnerable to attacks from nomads, but also free to expand across the Asian continent.

The fact that Russia was the only surviving independent bearer of Europe's indigenous eastern tradition is of utmost importance. The idea of Moscow as a "third Rome" naturally took over after the second's downfall. The vision of Russia as a third Rome created an idea of the state that was essentially imperial. Moscow grand dukes were still collecting the lands of the Northeast, but Russian czars went on to cast their aegis over all Orthodox Christians, whom they considered to be their natural subjects or wards. In the seventeenth and eighteenth centuries, the czars acquired nearly all the lands of the former Kievan Rus, and in the nineteenth, produced a concept of a single Russian nation comprising Great Russians, Little Russians (Ukrainians), and White Russians (Belarusians). From the eighteenth century, they had been eyeing Constantinople itself, first as part of Catherine II's Greek project, then under the guise of pan-Slavism, and later more frankly as part of a strategy that viewed the Near East as Russia's absolute foreign policy priority. Known as the "eastern question," this fixation has run as a guiding thread of Russian "close-to-home" imperialism.

As Europe's frontier nation, the Russians were not constrained on all sides, and could expand overland. They did, and built an empire of a different kind from the maritime powers of Western Europe and the German Reich. This Russian *derzhava* was definitely of European origin, but it spread beyond Europe in more than geographical terms: a sort of Europe Plus. At the same time, from the Mongols to Stalin, it experienced long periods of isolation and self-isolation from Western Europe.

The Mongols came just as Russian national identity started to emerge. "Shaking off the Mongol yoke" announced the birth of an independent Russian state. The two and a half centuries that lay between the Mongols' coming and going mark the period of Russia's gestation. This combination of a Christian "soul" and Asiatic political ways has forever stayed at the core of the Russian political identity. The Moscow grand dukes did not so much defeat the great Khans (or czars, as these Mongol rulers and the Byzantine emperors before them had been known in Russia) as succeed them and fully appropriate their legacy.

Muscovy, however, was not the only historical persona in Russian history. The aristocratic republics of Novgorod and Pskov represented for close to half a millennium a different version of medieval Russia, a trading northern European republic. Later, St. Petersburg and Moscow for 300 years stood for very different Russian attitudes to the Western world. Through all the continuities and inconsistencies in Russia's history, however, a few attitudinal and behavioral patterns stand out.

At the top of the list comes fierce insistence on independence from and equality with the strongest powers of the Western world. No sooner had Moscow liberated itself from the Mongol domination, than it took steps to assert itself as a European power. Status mattered a lot. Grand Duke Ivan III married a Greek princess and adopted Byzantium's double-headed eagle as Russia's state emblem. However, he declined a Holy Roman emperor's offer of a kingship, in order not to be regarded as the emperor's nominal vassal. Instead, the grand dukes proclaimed themselves czars, first informally, then in an elaborate act of coronation, by Ivan IV in 1547.

The Russian empire was born out of a war against northern Europe's premier military power, Sweden. The long Northern War (1700–1721) gave a major boost to Russia's modernization. Even before the war, Czar Peter (1672–1725) made a long journey to Europe. His immediate priorities were the army and later also the navy, but his truly enduring legacy was the founding of a modern state complete with a European-style government bureaucracy. Peter learned from the West and made others follow suit. Westerners held high positions in Russia, and Russians spent time in Western Europe as students. Peter the Great, the first emperor, became the role model of Russian westernizers. His central idea was to put Russia on equal footing with Europe's most powerful nations. His chief limitation was an exclusive focus on the state and his failure to fully appreciate private interests. And, of course, as Lenin had remarked before he himself had a chance to govern the country, Peter "used barbarity to fight barbarity."

From the early seventeenth century, major domestic crises in Russia invited Western powers to try to control it and reduce its territory and influence. The first Time of Troubles (1603–13) led to the Polish occupation of Moscow and the election of a Polish prince as Russia's czar; the second one, in 1917–20, inspired both German financial and logistical support for the Bolsheviks and the allied (the Entente, United States, and Japan) military intervention in Russia. The end of the Soviet Union ushered in a Russian Federation, which for a few years took its cue mainly from the United States and Western Europe.

The Time of Troubles also started the pattern of massive invasions from the West. The Poles were succeeded by the French (1812) and the Germans (1941). Each of those invasions put the fate of Russia in question, and each awakened the national spirit and a patriotic movement. The one monument in Moscow's Red Square is to merchant Kuzma Minin and Prince Dmitri Pozharsky, who liberated Russia from the Poles. In 2004, the day of their victory in Moscow (November 4) was elevated to a national holiday, replacing the anniversary of the communist revolution (November 7).

A useful way to look at Russo–Western relations is to compare them with Russia's relations with Asia. Not only was Russia invaded from the east as well as from the west, but for a quarter of a millennium it was part of political Asia. The Mongols were religiously tolerant and allowed for political autonomy. Russian princes had to offer their allegiance and taxes, and ask for investiture, but on their land their rule was supreme. This contrasted with the behavior of the Catholic crusaders, who sacked Constantinople in 1204 and later sought to baptize Novgoroders, whom they considered heathen. Thus, almost from the beginning, Russians found themselves "between the Mongols and Europe," assailed from both sides and having to assert themselves vis-à-vis the East as well as the West.

The early Russian princes were faced with an existential dilemma. It was resolved by Alexander Nevsky (1220–1263), whom the Russian Orthodox Church considers a saint. He defeated Swedish and German incursions, but chose to be subservient to the Mongols, spending years as a forced guest of the Khan. His priority was to fend off the threat of western (i.e., Catholic) assimilation. As to Asian political domination, he stoically accepted it. Alexander's successors followed suit, gradually gathering strength to overthrow the Mongol yoke, even as they married their Christian souls to Asian political practices.

Despite the centuries of servitude, Russia, unlike some of its smaller coreligionists, acquired no typical victim complex. It could not and would not appeal to the West (i.e., the Catholic Pope and the equally Catholic emperor) to engage in a crusade on Russia's behalf. It managed to liberate itself from the Mongols and then all others who had sought to dominate it. Instead of seeking help, Russians developed a defender complex, that of a nation shielding the West from common enemies, often without getting either a reward or even recognition. In Russian popular thinking, the medieval Russian principalities absorbed much of the Mongols' initial push and had greatly diminished their power by the time they reached Central Europe. Russia performed a public service to Europe again in 1812 when it not only defeated Napoleon in its own territory but went on to chase him all the way to Paris. In 1914, Russian armies helped relieve the German pressure on Paris, and in 1941–1944, the Soviet Union bore the brunt of the war against Nazi Germany.

In reality, across the board, Russia has been as much of a defender as an attacker. From the fifteenth through the seventeenth century, it struggled with Poland for domination in Eastern Europe, tried to gain access to the Baltic Sea, controlled by the German (Livonian) knights and later the Swedes—and sought to protect the southwestern approaches to Moscow from the raids of Crimean Tartars.

Due to its many peculiarities, which many mistook for absolute uniqueness, Russia has found it difficult to integrate or be integrated into the Western world. Early Western attempts at Russia's integration failed, because they were based on the West's supremacy. The papal offer to merge the Orthodox Church with the universal Catholic church was rejected in Moscow in 1439. A century and a half later, the leader of the Russian church, with only the czar's blessing, was proclaimed Patriarch of Moscow (1589), on a par with the nominal head of the Orthodox Church, the Patriarch of Constantinople.

Russia's early interaction with the West followed practical necessities. Moscow's monarchs invited in Western military men, who helped build a modern army; architects and craftsmen, who erected the Kremlin fortress and some of its principal cathedrals; and Western doctors, who treated the Russian royal family. Russia also entered the European system of power relations, initially as a fringe player. Much more important, but unfortunately generally unsuccessful, were the attempts at domestic reform, legally encoded, for example, in the Judgment Books of Ivan III (1497) and Ivan IV (1550). Both were domestic creations, rather than variations of Western statutes.

Thus, Russia was not joining the West, but instead tried borrowing some of its administrative, military, technological, and cultural achievements, while remaining sovereign within its own realm. As such, it demonstrated a strong desire to be treated as an equal by western Christians—while playing the part of the patron and protector of eastern Christians (eastern and southern Slavs, Greeks, Moldovans, Wallachians, Armenians, and Georgians). The future main axes of Russian foreign policy activism appeared some 500 years ago.

Russia's modernization drive was naturally inspired by a sense of military weakness vis-à-vis the West. If anything, Russian reforms were an attempt to catch up with the West. From the days of Mikhail, the first Romanov czar (1613–1645), Western military experts were called in to help upgrade the Russian army. Czar Alexei (1645–1676), Mikhail's son and the father of Peter the Great, made first steps toward building a navy. Diplomats like Ordin-Nashchokin and Artamon Matveyev were seeking to fit Russia into the European power constellation. Statesmen like Vasily Golitsyn prized Western learning and education. The city of Moscow boasted a lively colony of Western craftsmen, merchants, military experts, doctors, and others.

The Russian way of getting the West's recognition was to fight for it. Like the tsardom of Moscow, the Russian empire was self-proclaimed and not immediately recognized. It took western Europe about three decades after Peter's death to acknowledge Russia as a major continental player. Russia won that recognition chiefly by its participation in the frequent wars that were typical of eighteenth-century Europe. Russian armies took Berlin (1760) and crossed the Swiss Alps en route from northern Italy to Austria (1799), while the Russian navy defeated the Turks in the Mediterranean (1770).

Soviet Russia had humble social beginnings as a pariah state and thus a low start in international life. An unrecognized state for several years (Great Britain established diplomatic relations with the Soviet Union in 1924, and the United States only in 1933; the USSR was admitted to the League of Nations in 1934, only to be expelled in 1939), it had to make common cause with other pariah or rogue states of the time. Germany was its partner of choice, in both the 1922 Treaty of Rapallo and the 1939 Molotov–Ribbentrop Pact.

Russia competed with the major Western powers both inside and outside Europe. During much of the nineteenth century, Russia became Britain's main rival for domination in Persia and Central Asia. This came to be known as the Great Game. As Russia pursued the Great Game, the interests of trade and industry started to weigh ever more heavily. In the following decades, they would compete actively with the traditional geopolitical and strategic interests of the empire. One finds reflections of this in the U.S.-Soviet rivalry in the Middle East from the mid-1950s, culminating in the Soviet war in Afghanistan, but even more so in Russian–American rivalry on both sides of the Caspian Sea starting in the 1990s.

When Russia had recovered from the defeat in the Crimea and resumed its drive toward Constantinople in the 1870s, it faced another de facto coalition of Western powers, this time diplomatic. Again isolated, Russia had to give up much of the gains it had managed to extract from the Ottomans. The failure of its Near East diplomacy, in contrast with the victory of its arms, gave birth to Russian nationalistic rejection of the West as forever hostile. To be able to compete successfully against the West, Russian strategists came up with the idea of pan-Slavism. This called for uniting all Slavs under Russian aegis against the Romano-Germanic tribes of Western Europe.

In the aftermath of World War II, when the patriotic drive of the masses had evaporated and economic competition with the West became more difficult to sustain, military force and defense industry production became the chief currency of the Cold War on the Soviet side. Still reeling from the shock of the German invasion of 1941, the Soviet leadership vowed not to allow another surprise attack to happen again to their country. But they were certainly reaching for more, believing that military might would give the USSR an edge in the global competition. That resolve entailed building and maintaining a huge standing army, a powerful nuclear arsenal with a strong missile force, and a blue-water navy. In doing so, the USSR became a highly militarized state. Whereas other countries had a defense industry as part of the national economy, the USSR's civilian economy was an adjunct to the defense industry. Craving not only military security, but recognition, status, and power, the Soviet Union fought its way upward.

Its leadership believed they had reached their goal when the United States recognized strategic nuclear parity—essential strategic equivalence between the two countries. Dealing with different scenarios of nuclear war, however, naturally inspired caution and restraint. Starting with the 1962 Cuban missile crisis, the Soviet leadership displayed an interest in keeping the Cold War cold. This led to arms control agreements, signifying a mutual U.S.-Soviet interest in avoiding a major war between them.

While in military terms the USSR had become a status quo power, it still sought to undermine Western positions in the Third World. The 1970s witnessed the maximum expansion of Soviet power and influence. For the first time in its history, Russia became not only a military superpower, but also a truly global political power. It was deeply involved in the Middle East, South and Southeast Asia, Southern Africa, the Horn of Africa, and, disturbingly for the United States, in Central and South America and the Caribbean.

Soviet leaders felt flattered by Western references to the USSR as a superpower. For their part, they were fixated on the United States. The Kremlin developed a "summit-level mentality," focusing exclusively on the United States, with every other state almost out of sight. Europe was thought to be a mere function of the U.S.–Soviet relationship, effectively divided between the two and controlled by them. Asia was basically neglected. The Soviet leadership looked down on both China and Japan, deemed unfriendly, and India, a Soviet client, and saw much of the rest of the continent as an American–Soviet political battlefield. The Middle East was a focus of most bitter bilateral rivalry, the site of periodic proxy wars. Africa was up for grabs. The Soviets saw Latin America, a U.S. backyard, as the soft underbelly of the United States. Andrei Gromyko, who spent 28 years as the Soviet foreign minister, was the best exponent of this worldview.

On the military side, Soviet military commanders and defense industry captains were fully engaged in ever-intensifying military competition with the United States. Marshals Grechko, Ustinov, and Akhromeyev and Admiral Gorshkov built the largest military establishment in the world. Usually coming from behind, the Soviet Union kept up, simultaneously, with the United States, its NATO and non-NATO allies, and with China.

Competition and rivalry were the permanent features of the Cold War. Occasional crises intermingled with periods of détente, which usually led to new tensions. A crisis, unchecked, would have led to a war of universal annihilation. However, for the Soviet Union, there were inherent dangers in a relaxation of tensions. The last détente, which was allowed to run unchecked, brought the USSR down.

The Cold War was essentially the product of U.S.-Soviet competition. World War II is seen in Russia through the prism of the Great Patriotic War, the Soviet Union's struggle against Nazi Germany. The tradition of a one-on-one struggle with a major foreign, usually Western, enemy is dominant in Russian history. However, from the days of Peter the Great, who fought the war against Sweden with Poland and Denmark at his side, and Turkey aligned with the Swedes, Russia has had a long history of alliances and coalitions with Western powers. Under Peter's heirs, Russia was a member of many shifting alliances, making common cause with as many countries as it was challenging. By the late eighteenth century the Russian empire had become an inalienable part of the European international system. During the long reign of Catherine II (1762–1796), Russia was fully established as a European nation, rather than, like the Ottomans, an empire in Europe.

Alexander III, who succeeded his father after the latter's assassination by revolutionary radicals, was a reactionary at home and a proponent of splendid isolation abroad. ("Europe may wait," he proclaimed famously, "while the Russian czar is having breakfast.") However, geopolitical and economic reasons made this arch-monarchist welcome the French president to St. Petersburg in 1891 to the tune of La Marseillaise. In aligning itself with France and Britain against its fellow autocracies, Germany and Austria-Hungary, Russia demonstrated the dominance of geopolitical and economic factors over dynastic ties and ideological affinities. Thus, imperial Russia consistently displayed empathy for the democratic United States. During the American War of Independence, Catherine the Great proclaimed armed neutrality in 1780, which favored the Americans. During the American Civil War, Emperor Alexander II sent Russian warships to New York and San Francisco in a show of support for the North.

When Russia aligned itself with the more liberal Western countries, such as France and Britain, against more autocratic powers, such as Germany, Austria-Hungary, and Turkey, first within the context of the Entente, and then World War I, it had major significance domestically. Russian liberal westernizers sought to turn that alliance into an instrument of domestic change, while conservative quarters were plotting a separate peace and switching sides.

In Russia's relations with the West in the nineteenth and early twentieth centuries, its great-power façade obscured a much more primitive backyard. This combination of first-class military upside and third-rate social downside has continued as a salient and near-permanent feature of Russia as an international player. Behind the European façade of St. Petersburg, private property in the modern sense was still fledgling and established on the foundations of arbitrary rule and of serfdom, which was the lot of the majority of its population.

Even as Russia's power and influence grew, its domestic condition worsened. Alexander I's armies defeated Napoleon and entered Paris in 1814, and the Russian emperor became the founding father of the Holy Alliance and active in the Concert of Europe, which defended monarchical legitimacy and assured peace among all the principal nations. However, Russian military officers who had marched across Europe and seen conditions there attempted a coup in St. Petersburg in 1825 to abolish autocracy, introduce a constitution, and liberate the serfs. They failed, but their effort inspired a Russian revolutionary movement that fed upon the ever more radical ideas in Western Europe. Throughout Russian history, major victories against western powers often led to stagnation, while defeats resulted in upheavals and revolutions.

The abolition of serfdom (1861), about the time of the end of slavery in the United States, together with reform of the judiciary, municipal government, and the military, and other measures, amounted to the greatest step toward Russia's modernization. They were undertaken in the wake of the ignominious defeat in the Crimean War. With the growth of capitalism spurred by these reforms, Russia started to become Western for the first time beyond its army and government bureaucracy. Its foreign policy vis-à-vis the West became a policy of preparing for the lifting of the restrictions imposed after the Crimean War and the resumption of the drive toward Constantinople. In the Far East and Central

Asia, however, Russia went on an expansionist drive, citing a *mission civilisatrice* as Europe's cultural ambassador to backward territories and peoples.

From the mid-1990s, Russian foreign ministers have identified Alexander Gorchakov, head of Russian diplomacy after the Crimean War, as their role model. It took Gorchakov fourteen years to proclaim the Treaty of Paris, which ended that war, null and void. President Putin threatened to pull out of the Conventional Forces in Europe (CFE) treaty, which he called discriminatory against Russia, seventeen years after it was signed.

In much of Russian history, one can see a certain disdain for the "lands between," i.e., countries lying between Russia and the closest major Western power, Germany. Unimpeded contact with western Europe was made possible once Russia gained access to the Baltic and Black seas. Peter used force to establish control over the sea lines of communication from and to Europe, ending what had been a virtual transit monopoly for centuries controlled by Sweden, Poland, and Turkey. Peter's legacy is revered in Russia like no other, both by liberals and supporters of a strong state. There is also palpable abhorrence of another cordon that would isolate Russia from Western Europe, like the one broken through by Peter. Such a cordon, it is feared, would again make Russia dependent on its neighbors. The fear may be inordinate: there is no way that Russia can be physically isolated, but it is still real. This abhorrence is coupled with disdain that the Russian political class has for the former Soviet satellites, which, it believes, are destined to be somebody's wards: Moscow's yesterday, Washington's and Brussels' today.

Quite often, conservative Russia played the role of Europe's gendarme, whether on behalf of monarchical legitimacy or communist rule. As Russian influence in central and eastern Europe approached hegemony, after absorbing Finland and much of Poland into the empire, Emperor Nicholas I crushed a revolutionary movement in Hungary in 1848–1849. The Austrian monarch's gratitude was short-lived, but the image of an authoritarian eastern colossus as the gendarme of Europe was forever imprinted on the minds of European radicals and liberals. They soon joined with those, mainly in France and Britain, who sympathized with Polish insurgents in their periodic revolts against Russian rule. The Western public supported Poland's freedom on the principle of liberty, but the governments also sought to minimize Russia's international influence as a threat to the European balance of power.

Within Russian society itself, many a liberal saw the West as the preferable alternative to domestic autocracy. As early as the sixteenth century, nearby Western countries became an abode for Russian dissidents fleeing the wrath of the czar. These dissidents also formed a habit of corresponding with the powers-that-be in Russia, challenging them in matters of political philosophy and practical governance. From his Lithuanian exile, Andrei Kurbsky debated these issues with Ivan the Terrible, while Grigory Kotoshikhin, a century later, issued polemics from Stockholm. This tradition developed and flourished in the last 70 years of the Russian empire and during the 70-year life span of the Soviet Union. It has not vanished in post-Soviet Russia. Many liberals and democrats have looked to the West for inspiration and support.

The backlash in Russia against this Western-inspired liberalism often led to ultraconservatism's becoming mainstream and liberalism being lumped together with radicalism as antistate. While shutting off channels for legitimate debate and discussion, the tsarist government made a point of presenting itself to Westerners as "the only European in Russia." From the 1830s, Russian society split between those who rejected Peter's reforms and everything that followed it (Slavophiles), and those who supported modernization (westernizers). In different forms, this split has continued to this day. Yet, it would be wrong to regard the two groups as antagonists. There is room for dialogue, and some common ground. What both neo-Slavophile nationalists and latter-day westernizers must fear is a totalitarianism that grows out of populism. Such a regime, as the Bolsheviks demonstrated, would use Western technology but unleash an anti-modernist backlash to stamp out all dissent and all debate.

The link between war and revolution has been a recurrent theme in Russia. St. Petersburg's adventurous designs on the Far East brought about a rout at the hands of Japan and a revolution at home (1905). At last, Russia received a limited constitution, but since the state allowed no room for opposition, the opposition took on the state itself. Yet, in economic terms, Russia was making great strides. Given twenty years of domestic peace, which Prime Minister Pyotr Stolypin sought, Russia could have become a modern country with a viable economy by the early 1930s. This, however, was not to be.

World War I revealed and greatly exacerbated the weakness of the Russian state, which had critically retarded the development of the institutions such as mass property ownership and parliamentarism that would have provided stability and durability to Russia as a country.

Another major problem was referred to by Prime Minister Sergei Witte, who said that there was "no such thing as Russia, only the Russian empire." Ever since the days of Peter the Great, Russian travelers had headed to Europe, which was often in social turmoil. Nikolai Karamzin, the future great historian, visited Europe during the French Revolution. Soon after 1848, a revolutionary Russian émigré community sprang up in major European cities, including London, Paris, and Geneva. These Russian radicals, originally antigovernment, had no choice other than to be antistate. Spending decades abroad, they were losing touch with Russia even as their radicalism and impatience grew. While not particularly popular with the governments of the host countries, the émigrés were nevertheless tolerated, out of respect for freedom of speech, contempt for the czarist regime, which did not allow it, and in response to pleas on the revolutionaries' behalf from domestic (and much more moderate) socialists.

Lenin and Trotsky did not single-handedly "make" revolution in Russia. However, they and their Bolshevik cohorts, many of them with years or decades of European emigration behind them, made sure that the revolution turned radical and became the world's most spectacular experiment. It applied the teachings of a German economist and social philosopher to a vast country of which he had known little and never considered ripe for what he was preaching, i.e., communism. Those who sought to execute Marx's ideas soon turned into executioners. Roles changed. Suddenly, in Europe's and later America's eyes, three million defeated supporters of the *ancien régime* took the place of the few revolutionaries. For decades, the West became a home to the "other Russia," in fierce opposition to Moscow's communist rulers.

This tied in with Europe's own political problems with Russia. Nicholas I's ill-fated attempt to expand Russian influence in the Near East at the expense of the Ottomans led to a war in which Europe's major powers, Britain and France, backed Turkey and humiliated Russia by defeating it on its own territory, the Crimea. The defeat was particularly painful, because it had followed a half century of expansion after the triumphant patriotic war against Napoleon. It also revealed the deficiencies in Russia's internal organization far beyond the army's armaments and logistical system. The Crimean War ushered in a quarter century of reforms in Russia led by Alexander II. It is interesting that post-Soviet Russian foreign ministers, starting with Evgenii Primakov, have drawn parallels between Alexander II's reform period and Russia's current tasks. They have also rediscovered Alexander's foreign minister, Prince Gorchakov, as their role model. Gorchakov's most famous saying was:

"They say that Russia is angry. No, Russia is not angry. It is pulling itself together."

Isolation from without, however, was nothing compared to self-isolation. Despite Lenin's and Trotsky's efforts, Russia failed to spark a world anticapitalist revolution. However, the Bolsheviks endowed Soviet Russia with an ideology that put it into permanent conflict with the rest of the world and that at the same time became the principal legitimization of the regime and the state. Class-based and internationalist, the ideology of communism provided the Soviet leadership and its subjects with a uniform worldview and the only language in which they were permitted to express themselves. The Soviet Union, a profoundly conservative and hierarchical state, talked the language of the world proletarian revolution. The Soviet leaders did not mean everything that they were publicly saying, but they lacked an alternative means of expressing themselves.

In communist ideology, the "bourgeois West" became the ultimate "class enemy," an implacable social, political, ideological, and military foe. It was "the Other" of the Soviet system, and the antagonism was absolute. One system's loss was the other's gain. The USSR actually "created" the West under the rubric of "capitalist encirclement." This included all of Europe and North America. Fearful of communist propaganda and subversion, European countries responded by organizing a *cordon sanitaire* along Soviet borders. Very soon, any hopes of proletarian solidarity were dashed. The German "workers and peasants in uniform" marched into the Soviet Union in June 1941. However, even though the USSR could no longer rely on its "class friends," it continued to confront its "class enemies."

The Soviet Union believed in its manifest destiny. Even though the West was much richer and more powerful, the Soviets saw themselves as history's favorites. "We will bury you," Nikita Khrushchev told Americans matter-of-factly, even cheerfully. This was not meant as a dark threat, but rather as a statement of a scientifically established truth. Similarly, the publicly displayed slogans like "Communism will win" were not meant as a declaration of war on the West, or even as intimidation, but rather represented anticipation of the predetermined future.

However, Soviet leadership did not believe in the automaticity of even the things that were historically inevitable. It imposed a strict discipline on its subjects, so that they did not become corrupted by the West. The Cold War environment served that purpose perfectly. The Soviet Union remained a fortress even after it had expanded its influence to dozens of countries. Its regime enjoyed a double isolation: from within (like the Berlin Wall, which was built on East German territory as a barrier against potential escapees, not against outside attackers) and from without (a result of political-military confrontation with NATO). Periodic crises only strengthened the Soviet regime; what it abhorred were the occasional moments of détente. Relaxation of tensions with the West in 1955 facilitated Khrushchev's domestic thaw, which had to be abandoned to shore up the control by the Communist Party. Brezhnev's détente bargain included the Helsinki Final Act with its human rights dimension, which helped erode the rule of the Party in the Soviet Union and Eastern Europe.

The Soviet Union had a keen sense of vulnerability *tous azimuths*. It was born of a civil war, which had been preceded by a world war and was succeeded in short order by international intervention in Russia. It had no friends (workers' solidarity being exposed as a sham), but could count nearly every country as a potential enemy. Between the world wars, it was fearful of "provocations" along its borders. It interpreted Western appeasement policies on the eve of World War II as primarily an anti-Soviet ploy, designed to channel Nazi aggressiveness against the USSR. (Ironically and lamentably, this theme resurfaced in Putin's speech after the 2004 terrorist attack in Beslan.)

On the eve of the war, Stalin and his cohorts mistrusted *all* "capitalists," treated social-democrats as traitors, despised "spineless" liberals who failed to live up to their commitments, and preferred solid conservative adversaries. For a time, Stalin deluded himself that he could "read" Hitler as a fellow totalitarian. Germany's surprise invasion in 1941 caught the Soviet leadership unprepared and virtually unawares. This was a gigantic Pearl Harbor, leading to losses of millions in killed, wounded, and captured within weeks, enemy occupation of two-thirds of Russia's heartland, and a last-ditch battle on the outskirts of its capital.

The war's end was the biggest triumph the Soviet Union had ever known or would ever experience. It was a "nation," united by a patriotic idea and enjoying unparalleled prestige abroad as the primary liberator of Europe from Nazism. During and immediately after the war, the USSR was a member of the Big Three, alongside the United States and Great Britain, coordinating the joint war effort of the anti-Hitler coalition and planning for the postwar international system. Between 1941 and 1945, Stalin was an accepted and respected partner of Roosevelt and Truman and Churchill and Attlee.

The Cold War had many sources, but one of the most important was Stalin's fear that the system he had built inside the country would become fatally corroded by too much exchange with the outside world. As the Soviet Union's influence expanded far beyond its borders, contacts with the West were reduced to a bare minimum. Even newly established pro-Soviet regimes in eastern Europe were viewed with suspicion. There was a firewall within the Iron Curtain, and it was meant to ensure the stability of the Soviet regime.

Stalin's more optimistic heirs relented on this and allowed some contacts. Nikita Khrushchev in 1957 hosted an international youth festival, the first time in four decades that large numbers of Russians and foreigners were brought together under peaceful conditions. Leonid Brezhnev in 1975 signed the Helsinki Final Act, which contained obligations in the humanitarian field. Eventually, ordinary Soviet people, by watching films and reading translated books, listening to Western broadcasts, and visiting foreign exhibitions, could form a fairly good— and possibly a "grass-is-greener"—picture of "life in the West." A section of the elite became responsive to Western values and ideas, such as human rights, the rule of law, and democracy. This was a major contributing factor to the demise of the Soviet Union.

With communist internationalism failing, Eurasianist geopolitics started creeping back in after 1917. The revolution created its own émigré community, which existed in parallel with the Soviet state for three-quarters of a century. Traumatized by the experience of war and revolution, defeat and exile, a small group of Russian émigrés in Europe came up with a set of foreign policy ideas, which became known as Eurasianism. A central feature of the concept was its insistence on Russia's unique place in the world as a Eurasian (rather than European or "internationalist") power and a deep mistrust of the West. It saw the West as first a bitter enemy/distant ally, then an ineffectual supporter against the Bolsheviks, and finally as treating Russia, despite all its sacrifice for the allied cause, as a loser in World War I, while recognizing the Soviet regime as legitimate. Convinced that "the (Western) allies are all rascals," the Eurasianists put their faith in Russia's rise from the ashes as a major independent power. In this, they conveniently overlooked the domestic condition of the country. In the 1920s and 1930s, Eurasianist ideas were hardly important; they became more relevant when the forces that had chased their originators out of Russia finally petered out, and Russia reverted to capitalism, albeit carrying its Soviet legacy with it.

Even though revolutionary internationalism was a short-lived phenomenon, it ushered in a concept: globalism. Under the communist regime, the Russian worldview for the first time became global. Moscow became the headquarters of the Communist International. After the Second World War, this early ideological globalism was expanded into the political-military sphere. This is a lingering legacy. From the early 1990s, Russian leaders have been rejecting what they perceive as Western attempts to "cage Russia in" as a merely regional power. Moscow insists that its reach is truly global.

The End of the USSR: A Change in Continuity

Many factors were responsible for the collapse of the Soviet Union. The Soviet system started to mellow on March 5, 1953, the day of Stalin's death. Under Khrushchev, it gave its last brief hurrah of zeal. This would have been too late, even if Khrushchev had tried to change the system. Brezhnev presided over rising materialism, fast degenerating into corruption, cynicism, and paralysis. General Secretaries Brezhnev, Andropov, and Chernenko, dying in quick succession in 1982–1985, helped produce the image of a dying system. The growing weight of internal problems made the Soviet leadership seek initially a breathing space in the all-out arms race with the West.

Personalities matter, of course, and the Gorbachev factor played a role no one could have predicted. Gorbachev's attempt to revitalize a moribund system only hastened its demise, while at the same time ensuring its soft landing, instead of a much harder one probably a couple of decades later. Perestroika confirmed the impossibility of improving the Soviet economy, and glasnost delegitimized the Soviet political system. New political thinking undermined the very foundations of Soviet foreign, defense, and security policies, including the sacrosanct Communist Party monopoly on power. An attempt to construct a more perfect union of Soviet republics terminated the USSR, which could only exist as a de facto unitary state. Within five years, the house that Lenin and Stalin had built became a mausoleum.

The Reagan factor played a major role, but it was never decisive. Ronald Reagan revived America's military might and steeled its resolve, thus putting pressure on the Soviet Union and straining its resources. More importantly, however, he opened up the prospect of détente and massive arms reductions. This détente, coming from a position of strength, was the kiss of death for the Soviet system. It might have coped with a new arms race, for a limited period of time, but it clearly could not withstand the demobilization, which put into question the

Communist Party's mandate to govern. Once the outside pressure was gone, the system imploded. However, it was Gorbachev's decision to open up the country.

Gorbachev defied the iron rule of previous Soviet leaders, laid down by Stalin: only as much contact with the West as strictly necessary, and even then under tight police control. His long talk about the "advantages of socialism" was shot down by Margaret Thatcher's single blunt rebuttal: "What advantages?" Already in 1987, when this exchange took place, the bulk of ordinary Soviets were with Thatcher.

Gorbachev subscribed to ideas of capitalist/socialist convergence too late. Having abandoned former communist infallibility, he was now preaching the middle way, but his offer had no takers, for it had become irrelevant. The West had learned the lesson from both world wars, revolutions, and the Great Depression: capitalism expanded its economic, social, and political foundation. The Marxian standoff between the bourgeoisie and the proletariat was replaced by the majority of the population's joining the middle class. The Soviet system, by contrast, had been made perfect by Stalin, and any tinkering with it was fraught with fatal consequences for the system. Gorbachev did not realize that, and cheerfully went ahead. His slogan, "More socialism," resounded like a death knell to *real* Stalinist socialism.

This was a period of deep confusion, which affected not only Gorbachev. The Soviet Union loftily proposed "new thinking" to "the entire world" at the time when its power and influence were plummeting. The USSR suddenly became truly popular in the West for the first time since 1945, even as it was visibly disintegrating. Soviet policy planners were eyeing some kind of benign world condominium with the United States at the time when a totally new world order was dawning. Soviet foreign policy in 1988–1991 was a unique case of imperial dismantlement-turned-self-destruction, all in the name of common security, international cooperation, and universal human values. Ironically, Soviet Russia was founded on the grand illusion of communism, which led to untold losses and colossal suffering. Soviet Russia exited peacefully on another grand illusion, one that assured the brutal system built on force and intimidation a surprisingly soft landing.

The Russian Federation

One of post-Soviet Russia's founding myths was that it was returning to the family of Western nations after three-quarters of a century spent in communist captivity. According to this myth, Russia, a "normal European country" by pre-World War I standards, had been hijacked by a bunch of internationalist Bolsheviks and become their first and principal victim. A number of Russians refused to be kidnapped into communism and fought back, resulting in 3 million lives lost in a bitter civil war. However, the anti-Bolshevik forces were divided and poorly led, and Western democracies failed to render effective support. Later, the West recognized communist rule in Russia and only sought to isolate and contain the Soviet Union. In the grim decades that followed, the Russian people lost tens of millions in the GULAG, forced collectivization campaigns, provoked famines, and in the war that Stalin had failed to foresee. By the beginning of the 1990s, the founding myth went on, the Russian people had liberated themselves by peacefully shaking off communist rule, established a democracy, and returned to the family of Western nations.

Putin was much criticized in the West for calling the breakup of the Soviet Union the greatest geopolitical catastrophe. From 1989 on, a score of Soviet client states around the world were essentially left to their own devices, and Moscow's half a dozen satellites in Eastern Europe were magnanimously set free. Within five years, some 700,000 Soviet troops withdrew from positions they had held for half a century. All this culminated when 14 constituent republics of the Soviet Union itself were in part allowed and in part told by Russia to secede. Their independence came suddenly, almost effortlessly, and was endowed with more than generous borders and without political or economic strings attached. Historically Russian territories, such as Crimea and northern Kazakhstan, were recognized as belonging to Ukraine and Kazakhstan, respectively. About 25 million ethnic Russians suddenly woke up on the wrong side of the border. The Soviet army allowed itself to be divided into a dozen national formations. The more than 10,000-strong strategic nuclear weapons arsenal, and perhaps as many "tactical nukes," remained intact. Historically speaking, the old order was gone virtually overnight, and virtually unlamented.

Incredibly, while going through a most painful transition, with people's savings evaporating and inflation reaching a few thousand percent a year, Russia managed to maintain a minimum degree of civil peace. However, what followed communism in Russia could hardly be described as a democracy. Nor was Russia admitted into the family of Western nations.

The Yeltsin leadership, however, claimed that Russia emerged a victor from the Cold War. It ended tyranny and voted in democracy and did this bloodlessly and of its own free will. It voluntarily relinquished hegemony over others and gained free neighbors in place of disgruntled subjects. It replaced hostility with friendship in relations with the West and opened itself up to the world. It withdrew from the burdensome arms race and drastically slashed its defense budget and the armed forces: the threat of war had receded greatly. Russia could walk with its head high and count on recognition from other members of the international community. Such was both the rhetoric and the thinking.

At that time, Russia's wish was simply to belong. It applied for NATO membership, sought to become America's formal ally, and talked about joining the European Union. It agreed to discuss Japan's territorial claims so that the two countries could finally sign a peace treaty a half century after the end of World War II. All Western clubs were good for Russia, provided they recognized her status as a major power and allowed her to become a member of the board. It appeared that Russia had no interests that would clash with the interests of the West or even significantly diverge from them. That approach became associated with Andrei Kozyrev, who served as Yeltsin's foreign minister until early 1996. Within Russia, not everyone agreed with the "Kozyrev line." For almost five years after the fall of the USSR, foreign policy was a contentious matter within the elite.

In return for its good behavior, Russia craved a seat at the top table. It sorely wanted recognition and reward for what its leaders and elites saw as unparalleled generosity, i.e., unilaterally retreating, disarming, and setting others free. But it wanted this quickly. It did not wish to queue indefinitely in the clubs' antechambers and to be treated on a par with its former satellites or borderlands. Russia is not an Estonia, was the oft-used motto. It also did not accept Western-designed matrixes and timelines for change. It had done its work and waited for what it thought was its due.

Russia did indeed manage to advance, but only slightly. Like all former adversaries, it was invited to join the North Atlantic Cooperation Council (NACC), created by NATO late in 1991 as a discussion forum. It joined the International Monetary Fund (IMF) and the World Bank in 1992 and signed a Partnership and Cooperation Agreement (PCA) with the EU in 1994, which went into force three years later. It became a member of the Contact Group on the Former Yugoslavia in 1994, and joined NATO's peacekeeping operation in Bosnia, under direct U.S. command, in 1995. At the G7 Denver summit in 1997, Russia was finally admitted to the club that it had been attending as an observer since 1991. The same year witnessed the signing of the NATO–Russia Founding Act, which established a Permanent Joint Council.

Nearly all of these arrangements were useful, but, with the notable exception of the G7/8, none amounted to real integration. Basically, Russia almost immediately became a peripheral partner of the United States and Europe, which used international institutions and bilateral relations to manage its weakness and help soothe Russian wounds, but not to integrate it. Russia the great power was out, and a Russia of the regions, a loose confederacy of semi-independent territories, was on the way in. Or so people thought.

In less than a dozen years, Moscow's international power and role had greatly diminished. The Middle East, Latin America, and Africa disappeared from Moscow's radar screen, and so did much of Asia, with the notable exceptions of China and an almost virtual, placeholder-like relationship with India, once a major Soviet ally. NATO's eastward enlargement de facto removed Russia's influence in Central and Eastern Europe, and NATO's muscular peace enforcement and then its brief air war in the former Yugoslavia (Kosovo) effectively removed Russia from the Balkans. Even within the post-Soviet Commonwealth of Independent States (CIS), geopolitical pluralism was on the rise, with the GUUAM (Georgia-Ukraine-Uzbekistan-Azerbaijan-Moldova) bloc and the BTC (Baku-Tbilisi-Ceyhan) pipeline sapping Moscow's residual standing there.

In the 1990s, the Russian leadership played with several basic foreign policy options. These did not come in exact succession, but rather overlapped, disappeared, and reappeared. The first one was to become America's coleader, a friendly democratic superpower, a sort of vice president of the post-Cold War world. This option was shot down almost immediately. Yeltsin sent a letter to NATO heads of state in December 1991 telling them that Russia was considering applying for NATO membership in the foreseeable future. When NATO leaders failed to respond, Yeltsin sent them a second letter, saying that there had been a misprint in the original message: Russia was not considering membership anytime soon. Still undeterred, Yeltsin made a plea to George H. W. Bush in May 1992 to conclude a bilateral U.S.–Russian alliance. Bush answered that now that the Cold War was behind them, there was no need for such an alliance.

A second option was to join Europe, now embodied in the European Union. In his mid-1989 Strasbourg speech Gorbachev had already called for "a common European home." Four months later, Gorbachev allowed the communist East German state to collapse, and twelve months later he agreed to Germany's reunification under Bonn's leadership and within NATO. Spurned by the United States, in the 1990s, Russian leaders started stressing Russia's European vocation and began making references to Russia's desire to join the European Union. What they were able to get, after much wrangling, was membership in the Council of Europe, which came in early 1996, toward the end of the first military campaign in Chechnya. Within the council's parliamentary assembly, Russian actions in Chechnya soon became a prime target for scrutiny and criticism. Moscow's attempt to elevate the Cold War-born Conference for Security and Cooperation in Europe (CSCE), its long-term favorite, into the principal regional security organization, towering over NATO and the EU, had decidedly mixed results. The conference changed its name to "Organization," but it also changed its brief to a democracy and human rights watchdog, primarily east of the former Iron Curtain and mostly in the area of the former Soviet Union. Within the new OSCE, Russia felt increasingly isolated.

In just three years (1993–1996), NATO expanded to the east to include Poland, the Czech Republic, and Hungary, made its presence felt in the Balkans, fought a war in Europe (in Kosovo)—and all that not only without Russian consent but over Moscow's vehement opposition. By the summer of 1999, Russian influence was for all intents and purposes over in countries outside of the CIS. The notions of Europe and the European Union became basically identical. The EU's power of attraction created a kind of "near abroad," encompassing, especially after the "color revolutions" of 2003–2005, a new eastern Europe and the south Caucasus and opening into energy-rich Central Asia. Russia was the only country that resisted the general run to Brussels. Russia-in-Europe was being supplanted by Russia-and-Europe.

By the mid-1990s, Russian–Western relations were in deep crisis. Moscow's disappointment and resentment over its rejection by both the United States and the EU led to the rise of theories that posited Russia at the head of the non-West, the silent global majority. Ideas ranging from reestablishing a sort of Russia-led confederacy around the CIS, to forging a Moscow–Beijing axis, to striking a triangular alliance among Russia, China, and India had one thing in common They existed almost exclusively in Russian heads. In practice, the new stance amounted to allowing the regimes of Slobodan Milosevic in Serbia, Saddam Hussein in Iraq, Kim Jong-il in North Korea, and the Iranian clerics to manipulate Russia to withstand or stave off U.S. pressure.

Psychologically, this was a typical "Scythian" reaction, repeating the poet Alexander Block's famous lines written in 1918. The idea was that, spurned by Europe as "aliens," the Russians accept an "Asian" persona and turn into the West's implacable nemesis. This is a recurrent theme. In 2006, Gazprom CEO Alexei Miller and President Putin warned Europeans that failure to accept Russian terms for energy cooperation would lead Russia to redirect her oil and gas flows eastward. In other words, if Russia is pushed out of Europe, she will rediscover Asia. Over the decades, this apparent blackmail invariably failed.

A seemingly more realistic, though not very forward-looking, proposition was to embrace a version of neo-Eurasianism. To proponents of this idea, Russia stood as a unique bridge state, spanning the huge continent and naturally mediating between the East and the West, North and South. However, in the real world this stance would have necessitated an active imperial policy, for which Russia was woefully lacking in resources: the previous version of "Eurasia" had been the Soviet Union. This idea was finished in 2005, when Gazprom decided to stop subsidizing the new independent states, regardless of whether they were Russia's friends or foes.

A different version of Eurasianism was included in the concept of Russian–Chinese alignment and the work of the Shanghai Cooperation Organization. In both theory and practice, Moscow values good relations with China as a major asset in its global position. It is also very suspicious of what it perceives as U.S. attempts to "undermine" that relationship. Member states and observers of the SCO, President Putin pointed out in 2004, account for more than half of the world's population. However, Russia's share in the SCO total population is barely 5 percent. In 2000, Putin wondered publicly what language will dominate Russia's Far East in a generation's time. Since then, he has stopped speaking out on this issue, but he has apparently never stopped thinking about it. The level of the government's attention to Eastern Russia has grown significantly. So far, the Kremlin has not come up with a magic solution for its Far East and Siberia, but they are now permanently on its radar screen.

Between 2003 and 2005, Russia went through a fundamental foreign policy change. It rediscovered itself once again as a great power. This time, however, the claim is not based solely on military force and political influence, but also underpinned by economic factors. Well beyond oil and gas resources, the Kremlin sees Russia as a rising economic power. The current slogans read: "Russia's business is business" and "What is good for Gazprom (Rosneft, etc.) is good for Russia." Business means intense and constant competition. The Russian leadership, de facto board members of *Russia, Inc.*, does not shy away from competition. Neither does it shy away from using its comparative advantages to get a better deal from its Western partners, whether as principal energy suppliers to the EU or as operators of the Russian state inside Russia. The goal is to help Russian companies achieve prominent positions in the world's top league, while preventing a "takeover" of the most precious Russian assets by outsiders.

All this is anything but isolationism. Rather, it is an attempt at integration on one's own terms, working one's way through and up. Russia, Inc., wants to own European gas distribution networks and oil refineries, it buys up American steel mills and aluminum plants, and welcomes Japanese and Western carmakers to build factories in Russia. It allows only subsidiaries of Western banks but is open to Western insurance companies. The West, however, is not enough. It reaches out to China and Iran, South Africa, and Latin America, mostly as a competitor of American and European companies.

Having paid off its Soviet-era and more recent debts, Russia does not feel it owes anything to the West. It insists on equal status with the United States and the European Union and will not accept anything short of that. It rejects those who lecture it and talks back to them, sneering at their own flaws and failings. It stresses sovereignty, which it sees as a very rare attribute of just a handful of states, led by the United States and China, and has decisively rolled back foreign influence in Russian internal politics.

Russia has left the Western solar system, where it was farthest from the "sun," yet attracted to it by early hopes and long dependencies. It no longer wishes to be admitted to NATO and is not impressed by the workings of the European Union. It sees little practical interest in reaching out to the United States. It publicly berates Western-dominated bodies like the Council of Europe and the OSCE and hints at a growing loss of interest in their membership. Again, this is anything but isolationism. Moscow is prepared to do a deal with Washington, such as over Iranian or North Korean sanctions within the UN Security Council, but it expects a *quid pro quo* for each inch it moves its position closer to America's.

As a free agent, Russia looks beyond the traditional West and seeks to strengthen links to the leading emerging powers, from China and India to Brazil and Argentina to South Africa and Iran. The Shanghai Cooperation Organization has become a major Asian forum, in which Russia and China are coleaders, and the United States and the EU are not even observers. Within the former Soviet space, Russia has demonstrated the difference between an empire and a great power. It dropped integrationist illusions, and replaced them with economic expansionism with a full use of Russia's comparative advantages. In some cases, subsidies have been succeeded by sanctions. Very importantly, the Kremlin sees the former imperial borderlands as a sphere of its key interests, and actively seeks to reduce American, European (and also Chinese) influence there to establish Russia's clear primacy.

Conclusion

The post-Soviet evolution of Russian foreign policy is in keeping with many historical traditions. Russia is once again a stand-alone power. It resists assimilation and absorption into the West and abhors foreign domination. It wants equality with the world's premier powers. It seeks a friendly neighborhood in which it feels comfortable. While pursuing its interests, Russia can often be bullish, arrogant, even brutal. Those who carry out Moscow's foreign policy can be heavy-handed, openly biased, uncaring, narrow-minded, and stupid. In this, however, they are hardly unique in the world.

What is more interesting is that not all the features of current Russian foreign policy are old. Many are new, even revolutionary. Never before has a business interest played such a salient role in foreign policy making. Never before has the military security factor been so scaled down. The replacement of a faith-like ideology with pragmatism verging on cynicism is an often-made point in any discussion of present-day Russia. The country's reconstitution as a great-power nation state marks a clear break with half a millennium of imperial history.

Russia is in a postimperial phase of its existence. It does not seek to dominate the world, or to use its resources for some transcendental mission. Its failures, culminating in a collapse, have endowed it with valuable experience. Some of the lessons that the post-Soviet Russian leaders have drawn from their dealings with the West could be summarized as follows:

The world is based on an interplay of partial interests. There are no universal interests except for the survival of the human race. The currency in the interplay is power. While military power has not lost its significance as *ultimo ratio*, it is economic power, technological prowess, and cultural attraction that are of prime importance. International relations are about competition in power and mastery in employing it. To advance its interests, Russia must be strong and capable.

As a major country, Russia must be an independent actor. By definition, it can have no natural friends or sponsors. Instead, it has partners who are also competitors. Virtually anyone can be a partner, and practically anyone can be an opponent. The cooperation-to-competition ratio varies, depending on a particular field of interest, point in time, and wider constellation of power relationships.

Western talk on democracy and values is essentially hollow and is used to put American or European interests at an advantage and Russia at a disadvantage. Western powers routinely use double standards in approaching similar situations, depending on their particular interests. Compare the attitudes taken by the West toward the Belarusian versus the Turkmen regimes, or to the war in Chechnya versus Turkey's operations against the Kurdish rebels, and the "frozen conflicts" in Kosovo versus those in the former Soviet Union: Moldova/Transnistria, Georgia/Abkhazia, Georgia/South Ossetia, Nagorno-Karabakh.

In dealing with the United States, Russia should make sure all American promises are in writing and so legally binding. Moscow should never rely on Washington's good will. U.S. interests do not equal humanity's interests, so every concession to the United States requires reciprocity.

In dealing with the Europeans, the Russians should reach out to the key countries with the strongest interest in Russia, such as Germany, France, and Italy, and prevent the "new Europeans" from acquiring too much influence over the European Union's common stand toward Russia.

Russia's foreign policy continues to evolve. Unless there is a striking reversal in Russian domestic politics, however, the above features are likely to shape the substance and form of Moscow's foreign policy in its early-capitalist, post-imperial stage. Dealing with this Russia is a challenge that requires a fundamental rethinking of U.S. and EU approaches toward Russia. Such rethinking needs to be informed by an analysis of American and European policies since the fall of the Soviet Union.

CHAPTER 4

THE WEST
AND RUSSIA

American and European policies toward the Russian Federation were the continuation of their policies toward the Soviet Union in its terminal perestroika phase. Thus, it makes sense to discuss the Western approach to Gorbachev's USSR before analyzing bilateral relations in the post-Cold War period.

Many in the West, the United States especially, credit American policies, in particular those of President Reagan, with crushing communism, defeating the Soviet Union, and achieving victory in the Cold War. Reagan did reverse U.S. decline, he did press the Soviets hard: in Afghanistan, with missile deployments in Europe, and with his strategic defense initiative. Yet, Reagan's major contribution to the end of the Cold War and the defeat of communism can be traced to his decision to use the new U.S. position of strength to pursue open-ended détente, without mentioning that much-discredited word, with the Soviet Union. As the previous chapter has argued, the Soviet Union thrived in enclosure and died of exposure.

Western Europeans, while treading softly, generally followed the U.S. line, but were, at times, more enthusiastic about or more skeptical of the Soviet Union. In the 1960s, President de Gaulle's vision of a Europe stretching from the Atlantic to the Urals came to be seen as a powerful statement. In the 1970s, Chancellor Brandt's *Ostpolitik* provided a framework for close practical engagement between West Germany and the USSR. In the 1980s, following her adviser Professor Archie Brown's lead, Margaret Thatcher was the first Western leader to identify Mikhail Gorbachev as a leader to be closely engaged, but she would not hear of the suggestion that nuclear weapons could be abolished. As to John Paul II, the Polish pope, his enormous impact on his native country and others in Eastern Europe notwithstanding, his role in undermining the Soviet regime itself was modest. Generally, the Western Europeans saw early attempts at perestroika as an attempt to relaunch the Soviet economy and glasnost as more sophisticated public relations for the ruling Communist Party. Their general view was that a younger and more energetic Soviet leader was trying to revitalize an ossified system. New style, perhaps, but stale substance.

Both early American and Western European goals regarding Gorbachev's USSR were essentially conservative. At a minimum, they sought to keep the Soviet Union in its box and make it pay more, in blood and treasure, for the mischief it had created across the world. The hapless Afghan war gave them a big opportunity. At most, and more benignly, they considered capitalizing on the Soviet need for a breathing space and on the relative openness of the younger Soviet leadership, which they hoped would make the USSR more amenable to dialogue with the West and more predictable as an international actor. Even the German *Ostpolitik*, the most advanced Western policy initiative toward the East, made it clear that *Wandel durch Annaeherung* (change through rapprochement) applied only to Soviet-dominated East Germany. Gorbachev and his more liberal advisers were disappointed at Reagan and his colleagues' caution about reviving détente when the two leaders first met in Geneva in November 1985.

The U.S.–Soviet Reykjavik summit of October 1986 was probably the turning point. Gorbachev and Reagan failed to agree on the abolition of nuclear weapons, but they established a mutual rapport. The wider context was hugely important. In 1986, oil prices fell sharply, and the Soviet economy started showing serious strain. The Soviet leadership took a fateful decision, against which it had been warning its Eastern European clients for years, to begin borrowing in the West on a large scale. Inevitably, due to this indebtedness, Soviet foreign policy *had* to become more accommodating, from the arms race to Afghanistan. At the same time, Soviet domestic liberalization went beyond all former "thaws," featuring ever-more-open debates, and ever less-controlled media. Western leaders took account of the changes, but they largely interpreted them as tactical maneuvering, undertaken under duress. The Soviet system still looked impregnable and impervious.

The following year, 1987, was crucial. Gorbachev made a fatal attempt to revitalize the Communist Party by introducing elections in the party. Elections delivered a crushing blow to the system, for divisions within the Soviet leadership came into the open as political and ideological struggle, rather than jockeying for position. Tinkering with the Soviet economy by introducing market principles without a fundamental reform undermined it and, for practical purposes, legalized private entrepreneurship. Glasnost spun out of control and strove toward freedom of speech, still taboo. The USSR then crossed a major foreign policy threshold. It announced a readiness for deep and asymmetrical arms reductions under close inspection, starting worldwide strategic retrenchment, disguised, of course, as redeployment. This constituted a qualitative change, which was appreciated in the United States and Western Europe.

It was at this stage that the West became actively involved with Soviet transformation. It frankly aligned itself with the communist liberals: foreign minister Eduard Shevardnadze, glasnost architect Alexander Yakovlev, and Gorbachev himself. Still, the U.S. goal was a Soviet Union "lite," i.e., less threatening externally and more liberal ("revisionist," as communist hard-liners would put it) domestically, a bit like Deng Xiaoping's China in the 1990s. West Germany's objective was to ease the division of Germany and reduce military confrontation in Central Europe. Britain sought more engagement to further erode the vicious communist system, and France was thinking through new versions of pan-European détente. It was also at that time that the issue of Central Europe ("Mitteleuropa") suddenly surfaced in politico-academic debate, the implication being that the time was getting right to work for its neutralization, or "Finlandization."

By 1988, the Soviet leadership had become heavily dependent on Western loans. Its foreign policy essentially started to eschew any confrontation with the West. In the new military doctrine, "defense sufficiency" was no longer a hollow phrase. Armed forces started to be cut in earnest. Soviet troops headed for the exit in Afghanistan, heralding the end of the Soviet "outer" empire. Even then, few believed it would unravel so soon. Meanwhile, domestic strains came near the breaking point. Ethnic violence erupted in the borderlands. Gorbachev announced reform of the state, in effect undermining the Communist Party's monopoly on power. It was at this point that a reactionary backlash, had it come, might have had its last chance of success. It never came.

Probably feeling rather than fully understanding that, Western leaders tried hard to secure their gains, while the liberal phase still lasted. Most did not believe Gorbachev's policies would endure or prevail. Western objectives at the time, however, did not reach beyond extracting as many concessions as possible from the embattled Gorbachev administration before the window of opportunity closed. These concessions, enormous by Cold War zero-sum standards, were, in fact, clearly limited. They did not entail, e.g., the dissolution of the USSR. Besides going through with massive nuclear and conventional arms cuts, the Soviet Union had to cede most of its assets in the Third World and significantly ease its control in Central and Eastern Europe. Still, months before the fall of the Berlin Wall, Cold War inertia was as strong as ever. When George H. W. Bush succeeded Reagan in January 1989, he paused for several months to review relations with the Soviet Union. Right through 1991, the Pentagon published brochures on *Soviet Military Power*. Meanwhile, the Japanese, steeped as they were in the Cold War mentality, never fully recovered from their early skepticism while the USSR still survived, and missed a chance to persuade Gorbachev to give up the disputed southern Kuril Islands.

Revealingly, it is 1989 and not 1991 that is now widely regarded as the end of the Cold War. Central and Eastern Europe were set free, with virtually no strings attached, pursuant to Gorbachev's "Sinatra doctrine": do it your way! Poland initiated an ongoing "roundtable" dialogue on power sharing between the government and opposition and swore in its first noncommunist prime minister. East Germans fled across the hole in the Iron Curtain that was Hungary. People broke through the Berlin Wall with Soviet troops standing by, and Gorbachev saying, as if at the funeral of communism in Eastern Europe: "Those who come too late are punished by life."

At the Bush–Gorbachev meeting off the coast of Malta in November 1989, the post–World War II European order was laid to rest: Come Malta, exit Yalta. For the first time, Europe was practically whole, at peace, and virtually free. Within a year, Germany was united, *presto*, because no one could predict when the window in the Kremlin would close. Moscow finally "turned its key" on German reunification, but instead of a neutral Germany, which would have dramatically eroded U.S. geopolitical standing in Europe, it had to agree to a united Germany in NATO. Essentially, the West declared the Cold War over and celebrated victory with the Soviet Union still intact.

George H. W. Bush made his announcement of a new world order with regard to the Persian Gulf War, not the Berlin Wall (the infamous wall had just fallen on his watch). As the Soviet Union was unraveling, Western leaders started looking beyond the USSR. The remaining business from the Cold War was to ensure that the Soviet Union landed softly and that it agreed to sweeping arms reductions under the Conventional Forces in Europe (CFE) and Strategic Arms Reduction (START) treaties, which included provisions for intrusive inspections and other confidence-building measures (CBM).

There was no ambition to embrace a noncommunist Russia (or other republics, with the exception of the three Baltic states) that would emerge out of the collapsing Soviet Union. Almost right to the end, Western leaders preferred to deal with Gorbachev, not Yeltsin. (There were dissenters, notably in Cheney's Pentagon). They all expected and feared a reactionary coup in Moscow. When the putsch came, in August 1991, the United States and its allies were ready to deal with the coup leaders as the new authority in the Soviet Union. What happened in Moscow in August was no less than a miracle. Within three days, the putsch unraveled and its leaders were arrested; Yeltsin, first defiant, turned triumphant; and Gorbachev, returned to "a different country," as he admitted, was constrained to sign a decree, in front of TV cameras, banishing the Communist Party.

Thus, in the final years of the Soviet Union the West was cautious and conservative, yet pragmatic in dealing with the collapsing Soviet state. Western leaders didn't understand fully what was going on, and where it would lead. They preferred to err on the safe side. Events were moving too fast. They prudently avoided making far-reaching commitments to Gorbachev or codifying them when they made promises privately. The United States sought to limit Soviet military power and Moscow's global influence. Germany worked toward easing the division, and then ultimately overcoming it. Other Europeans hoped to see a "Finlandization" of Central and Eastern Europe. As soon as the Cold War was over, the USSR, on its deathbed, was put on a back burner, except for the issue of the Soviet nuclear legacy. Other problems quickly came to the fore: Iraq for the United States, Yugoslavia for the Europeans, and the Muslim world and China for both.

American and European Approaches toward Russia (1991–2006)

Russia was never a centerpiece of the West's post-Cold War agenda. American and European leaders felt relieved at the collapse of the Soviet Union, but did not feel obligated to its successors. There was no political, economic, or strategic need to integrate Russia at all costs, and doing this on Russia's terms was simply unacceptable. In 1989–1991, no new barbarian stood at the door to succeed Soviet communism. China was opening up, the Tiananmen clampdown notwithstanding, and not preparing to pick up the mantle of the fallen Soviet Union. Other issues were coming to the fore, pushing Russia to the side. NATO, in order not to go out of business, started to look for a new role. The European Union was embarking on a dual adventure of deepening and widening, i.e., further integration and enlargement. The United States went on to enjoy the fruits of globalization. The Western public's focus on Russia turned out to be extremely short-lived.

The lowering of the Soviet flag from the Kremlin on Christmas night 1991 was much less of a symbol of change for the West than the fall of the Berlin Wall. However, most people were thrilled, and there was a fair amount of general good will toward the new Russia. The suspicions of Russian reactionaries about the "perfidious West" were baseless. Neither America nor Europe had been anti-Russian in principle, however much they were anti-Soviet and anticommunist. Even so, there was no plan to destroy the Soviet Union or to break it up. There was also no plan on how to deal with the aftermath of the USSR's disintegration. Western leaders were thinking about holding their own in the confrontation, preventing a nuclear war, and ensuring a modicum of stability. They could not believe that on their watch they would face the issues of transformation of former enemy societies and their integration into the West.

With regard to Russia after communism, the West has practiced three distinct approaches, decline management, transformation assistance, and association.

Decline Management
The collapse of the Soviet Union was the first case in which a nuclear superpower disintegrated. The potential risks of WMD proliferation were enormous. Centralization of the former Soviet nuclear arsenal in Russian hands became an immediate top priority, mainly for its fellow nuclear superpower, the United States.

Linked to this objective was achieving ever deeper and more stabilizing cuts in the Soviet (and U.S.) strategic nuclear arsenals and parallel stabilization measures in tactical nuclear weapons.

Just a notch below that came implementing conventional arms control agreements, complete with confidence-building measures and verification mechanisms. A major priority here was completing Russian military withdrawals from Central and Eastern Europe and the Baltic states.

Managing Russia's decline included attempts to help the Russian elite absorb the immense shock of state collapse and status change. Even as Western leaders rhetorically embraced their Russian counterparts as new democrats, they continued to play to the Russians' wish to continue to be treated as leaders of a great power, second perhaps only to the United States.

In Russia's chaotic environment, Western capitals pragmatically decided to support President Yeltsin rather than promote institutional development. The approach of supporting democratic norms made little sense when the Russian parliament was dominated by communist and nationalist forces. Besides supporting Yeltsin's policies, including the more controversial ones, such as using force to suppress the parliament-led rebellion of nationalist demagogues, and to stamp out separatism in Chechnya, Western leaders sought to personally cultivate the Russian president, arranging frequent summits with him and keeping direct lines of communication open. The personal relationships that Clinton, German Chancellor Helmut Kohl, French President Jacques Chirac, and others established with Yeltsin worked as the principal guarantee that Russia would stay with the West, rather than stray from it.

At the same time, the United States in particular made sure that Russia remained unproblematic for the West in terms of its foreign policy. As a matter of principle, Russia was not given a de facto veto over NATO's decisions. The West spent some time and effort convincing Russia that its opposition to NATO enlargement of the Kosovo war was wrong, but the most that Western countries were prepared to do was to sweeten the pill for Russia. They proceeded regardless, even going around the UN Security Council before striking at Serbia in 1999 to avoid Russia's formal veto in that organization.

Russia's weakness and dependence on Western credits made it possible for the West to go ahead and consolidate the post-Cold War order in Europe without having to accommodate Russia beyond what was considered reasonable. Central and Eastern Europe, including the Baltic states, were integrated into European and Euro–Atlantic institutions. The Balkans became an area of NATO, and later EU, responsibility.

The United States and, much later, the EU reached out to the new states that emerged on the former borderlands of the Soviet Union. The United States immediately opened diplomatic relations with all of them and played a major role in shaping these new states' relations to the former metropolitan power, Russia. In some cases, the United States could even mediate between Russia and the others. Through its practice of geopolitical pluralism, sovereignty support, and multiple pipelines from the Caspian Sea, the United States effectively resisted Russian attempts to carve out a sphere of influence in what had been the USSR.

In the late 1990s, when Russian decline threatened to enter a new phase that might turn Russia into a virtual confederacy, the West started thinking seriously about the effects of Russian regionalization. Some were already thinking about a "world without Russia."

This policy of decline management lasted about a decade. Its results are fairly successful by the West's lights. Russia did not spread nuclear arms. Its nuclear weapons were placed under centralized control. Moscow adhered to its arms control commitments, even when those commitments were seen in Russia as one-sided and unfair (i.e., with regard to the CFE and START-2 treaties). Russia withdrew its forces from former Soviet outposts. The Yeltsin administration raised a hue and cry over NATO enlargement and NATO's air war in the Balkans, but it did not break with the West. Moscow accepted the establishment of the new states of the ex-Soviet Union, which many in Russia considered unfair, and did not try to politically exploit the issue of Russia's new diasporas resulting when Soviet-era administrative boundaries were turned into international borders. Eventually, Russia itself managed to stay in one piece, thus relieving Western statesmen of the challenge of dealing with chaos spreading over eleven time zones.

Transformation Assistance
Before the West started giving Russia technical assistance to facilitate reform, it had launched a major effort to provide humanitarian support. In the final months of the Soviet Union and in the first year of post-Soviet Russia, the United States and Western Europe shipped food, medicine,

and clothing. This averted major social problems: when the Yeltsin administration took over from Gorbachev's in December 1991, the country had only a few days' supply of food, and its currency reserves, at some 6 billion dollars, were at a historic low.

Western banks continued to give loans to Moscow, now under the Russian tricolor. For many years, promises of loans and conditions linked to them became the principal practical issue in Western–Russian relations. The Washington Consensus of the principal international financial institutions became the basis for Western recommendations to the Russian government, which it could ignore only at its own peril. In terms of its economy and finances, Russia was placed by its creditors under close supervision.

Western governments' support for Boris Yeltsin rested on their conviction that he was the ultimate guarantor of continuing reforms and the principal backer of reformist forces in his government. Yeltsin had virtually no political base left. His re-election in 1996 was the work of the Kremlin and the oligarchs; the West played along with that.

Again, even before the USSR had gone under, the West began giving the Russian government advice and assistance in drawing up programs of economic reform. This was later expanded into a massive advisory group of Western economists who helped fashion guidelines for finance policy and macroeconomic policy, privatization, and creation of a stock market.

A large number of Russians were admitted to American and European business schools, where they could for the first time study modern economics, business, and finance. This was perhaps the most serious foreign action to encourage self-help. The country, which in the late 1980s had had barely a handful of people knowledgeable about modern economics and even fewer practitioners, possessed thousands within a few years. In the early-to-mid-1990s, these people managed the biggest privatization process in history, which, notwithstanding criminal abuse and colossal waste, laid the foundation of private property in Russia. In 1997, Russia had the world's fastest-growing emerging stock market.

Besides providing economic and financial expertise, Western governments and NGOs gave Russia support in other reform fields: constitutional, legal, government and administrative; military, and public security. Visitation programs mushroomed, ranging from special "re-education" courses for flag officers at Harvard and in Germany to youth exchanges. Seminars, conferences, and lecture series were held across Russia. All relevant Western books, from the classics to the newest releases, were translated into Russian. The Russian expert working group tasked with writing the country's first democratic constitution, adopted in 1993, received all possible advice and drew heavily on American, French, and German experience.

Russia's fledgling civil society received support from Western grantmakers. The Ford Foundation, the MacArthur Foundation, and the Open Society Institute, to name but a few, established permanent presences in Moscow. The German political party foundations—Ebert, Adenauer, Naumann, and Boell—opened offices there. The Carnegie Endowment for International Peace created a branch in Moscow, which served as a model for future Russian think tanks. Russian NGOs, such as Soldiers' Mothers, received encouragement and support chiefly from European funders. The Moscow School of Political Studies, which offers courses for young civic leaders from across the country, received support from both U.S. and EU sources.

All this was very useful. In an unprecedented manner, Russia opened itself up to the West. The West, for its part, shared its basic expertise with its former communist rival. Even as the Russians hoped to catch up with Western Europe and the United States, Americans and Europeans hoped that the Russians, now that they had left communism behind, would become more like them. However, this engagement had limits. There was no debt write-off: Russia had to pay its Soviet-era debts. For both the Western creditors and the young Russian reformers, this was a matter of principle. There was no Marshall Plan either. The time for large-scale, government-backed, financial rehabilitation projects was over. Moreover, unlike Western Europe in the late 1940s, Russia half a century later was not deemed vital to U.S. national security.

It was not a defeated country, either, in the image of West Germany or Japan. It never formally surrendered its sovereignty. It was not occupied and ruled by a Western military administration. The pillars of the old regime, the Communist Party *nomenklatura*, the Soviet government senior bureaucracy, the managers of the state-controlled Soviet economy, and, in particular, its military–industrial complex, the security services apparatus, and the military officer corps all made the transition from the USSR to the Russian Federation. Three-quarters of a century after the Bolshevik coup, there existed no counter-elite to take over from the old Soviet one. Rotation and evolution, rather than revolution, was the name of the game. This was different from East Germany, Poland, and the Baltic states. It was also different from Romania and Bulgaria, where the similarly unreformed elites accepted unquestioningly U.S. primacy and EU rules. Russia insisted on rules of its own making and was, indeed, given special treatment, but not the one its leaders would have preferred.

Association Instead of Integration
Rather than integration into the West, the model that American and European policies pursued with regard to Russia was association with it. Moscow received invitations to join a plethora of Western-led forums, from the Council of Europe to the G7-turned-G8. These were loose associations, predicated on some notion of common values. Membership was meant to give Russia a place in the world at the side of the West and the role of a partner and co-contributor to Western causes. Americans and Europeans hoped that eventually Russia would become more deeply anchored to them and eventually grow into a reliable partner. That said, any talk of Russia's accession to the European Union would be absolutely premature, and any talk of a U.S.-Russian security alliance, irrelevant. NATO would nominally hold its door open to Russia, but as a practical matter focus on the nuts and bolts of defense reform.

This bottom-up approach contrasted starkly with Russia's traditional top-down one. In the 1990s, when Russian elites wanted integration in principle, they dreamed of an instant accession to a position of prominence within each and every club they were seeking to join. Instead of going through obligatory and tedious homework on the path to joining, they hoped to use networking to reach a master deal with American and European elites. This approach went nowhere.

The resulting compromise did not really make either party happy. Russia got a voice but no veto. Throughout the 1990s, Western governments enjoyed some influence in Moscow, but Russia refused to recognize U.S. leadership and become a follower. In the all-important case of Russia's cooperation with international financial institutions, both sides engaged in a game of mutual pretending. The IMF laid down the macroeconomic "party line" of the Washington Consensus, which the Russian government nominally accepted. This allowed for stabilization credits, which the Russians used as they saw fit, with Western monitors looking the other way. This unseemly cooperation ended after the 1998 financial crash.

In the political field, the Western leaders' apparently close personal relationships with Boris Yeltsin were poor compensation for Russia's continuing loss of standing and prestige. Russia's membership in the G8 was meant to offset the shock it received as three of the Soviet Union's former satellites joined NATO and to keep Russia at the West's side. At the time, this was a typical example of political expediency. Russia clearly did not meet the membership criteria: it was neither an established democracy nor a leading industrial power. There was hope, of course, that some day it would be both, but that day was well over the horizon. What mattered most to President Clinton and others was to give Yeltsin and his associates a sop to get over their post-imperial qualms.

In the absence of appropriate institutions, summit diplomacy played a key role. Beginning in 1998, the French and the Germans sought to achieve the goal of "anchoring" Russia by designing an informal, top-level, triangular relationship with the Kremlin to discuss a broad set of issues, but, more importantly, to underline Russia's European vocation. The idea was that Russian leaders would feel more comfortable and relaxed among "fellow Europeans" than in the increasingly unequal relationship with the only superpower. Even though this initiative received, at best, lukewarm support from Washington, it went in the same direction as America's own moves. Only briefly, in the 2003 run-up to the Iraq war and shortly thereafter, did the Paris–Berlin–Moscow "axis" really annoy Washington, and then more because of the roles played by Paris and Berlin than by Moscow.

In practical matters, Americans and Europeans engaged Russia on the range of international political and security issues through a number of special "half-house" mechanisms. During the Balkan crises of the 1990s, the Contact Group for the Former Yugoslavia resembled a latter-day concert of great powers deciding the fate of a volatile region. The 1997 NATO–Russia Founding Act established a consultative permanent joint council. This body was unable to thrash out Western–Russian differences over Kosovo and was practically abandoned. When the relationship was repaired and even grew closer in the wake of the 2001 terrorist attacks, a special NATO–Russia Council (NRC) was launched. It ostensibly placed Russia on equal terms with all its NATO partners, rather than making Russia face a common Western front. The NRC soon became a useful tool for practical cooperation—a Western ideal—though on a very limited range of technical issues, and did not lead to higher planes.

It looked as if, in late 2001 and early 2002, the United States and Russia would at last be able to establish a meaningful strategic partnership.

Common opposition to international terrorism appeared to unite the two countries as they had not been since the end of World War II. They even agreed to form permanent, high-level groups to coordinate their efforts in the global war on terror. Within months, this plan turned out to be hollow. The broader terms of cooperation were never agreed upon. Moscow was concentrating on its interests in the former Soviet Union and demanding that the United States abstain from undercutting it there. Washington refused and increasingly focused on Iraq.

On economic issues, the United States briefly pursued an intergovernmental commission format. Led by Vice President Albert Gore and Prime Minister Victor Chernomyrdin, the commission was hailed as an engine of commercial, technological, and economic cooperation. It inspired several clones, including one between Russia and France, before it went down amid the debris of the 1998 Russian economic crash. This model was never revisited, since Russia rebounded. Instead, Western governments sought to promote positive changes in Russia's economy. In 2002, the United States and the EU recognized Russia as a market economy. In 2006, the EU and the United States finally completed bilateral talks with Russia, paving the way for its entry into the World Trade Organization (WTO), which Moscow had been trying to join since 1994.

As far back as 1994, the European Union concluded a partnership and cooperation agreement with Russia, which opened the long-term prospect of a free trade area between them, but no membership. A decade later the EU and Russia agreed on a road map leading to the creation of four common spaces: economy and trade; justice, freedom, and security; external security; and research and education, excluding culture. These goals are broadly defined and provide for no timeline in achieving them. One element lacking in EU–Russia relations is conditionality. Membership in the EU is neither sought by Moscow nor offered (even as a long-term prospect) by Brussels. However, there is a fundamental point of contention: even as the EU treats Russia as a neighbor among others, as part of Europe's geographical environment, the Kremlin refuses to be an "object" of EU policies and insists on strict equality, as if between two major power centers.

When in 2001–2002 the idea of an energy partnership came up, it soon became clear that the U.S. and Russian governments had very different views of the content of the partnership. To many Americans, the idea was buying big into the Russian oil industry; to the Kremlin, the partnership was about gaining a foothold in the U.S. domestic market. Similarly with the EU countries: while the EU sought security of energy supply, the Kremlin was concerned about security of demand. The 2003 attack on the YUKOS oil company marked a watershed in Russian–Western energy relationships. The Russian government stepped boldly into the energy business, which it regarded as strategically important. The Kremlin utilized Russia's abundance of oil and gas to underpin the country's new claim to energy power status.

Russia's debut in the role of an energy power was staged in 2005–2006, as Gazprom withdrew subsidies from the former Soviet states, raised prices sharply, and even briefly cut off supplies to Ukraine. At the time, Georgia suffered when a gas pipeline from Russia was sabotaged by unidentified perpetrators. In 2007, in another pricing dispute, Russia stopped pumping oil to Belarus. This, in turn, raised fears in the EU and the United States about Russia's use of the "energy weapon" to beat its weaker neighbors into submission, which would also jeopardize Europe's energy security. Russia's stellar reputation as a reliable supplier was severely damaged. Domestically, energy nationalism triumphed. Western majors had to cede majority stakes in oil and gas projects to Russian state-controlled companies, and Gazprom refused to share the giant Shtokman gas field in the Barents Sea with anyone. Energy partnership turned into energy tension.

In the military sphere, what the West celebrated as a major achievement, namely, a Russian brigade's participation in the NATO-led operation in Bosnia-Herzegovina, was perceived as a disgrace by the Russian defense establishment. The nominal placement of a Russian unit under the top U.S. military commander in Europe, even through his Russian deputy, was branded an anti-model, something to be avoided. In contrast to that 1995 arrangement, in 1999 Russian paratroopers actually competed with NATO for the seizure of an airport in Kosovo, even at the risk of clashing with Western forces. The Russians demanded a separate sector of Kosovo. When the Western powers refused that, the Russians soon lost interest. In 2003, all Russian military peacekeepers were withdrawn from the Balkans.

What Went Wrong (If Anything)?
As mentioned previously, the post-Cold War Russian–Western interaction has had invaluable results. Russia has become undeniably capitalist, relatively open, and reasonably integrated into the world. Yet, both in Western countries and Russia there is a fair amount of unease. Since the publication in 1999 of the Cox Commission report to the U.S. Congress, and through the appearance in 2006 of the Council on

Foreign Relations report on *Russia's Wrong Track*, Republicans and Democrats have been exchanging criticisms about the other party's administration's dealings with Russia. Senior Russian figures, for their part, complain privately that the United States ignored their material concessions and spurned their sincere overtures.

The answer most frequently given to the question "What went wrong?" is that expectations were too high. True, many Westerners hoped too soon to see Russia as "one of us" in terms of societal values, economic organization, and political behavior. Similarly, too many Russians hoped that the arrival of "democracy" and friendly assistance from America and Western Europe would help them reach an average European standard of living *and* restore Russia's international pre-eminence. These expectations were both fairly widespread and wildly unrealistic, but they hardly drove policies in Washington, Paris, Berlin, or Moscow.

Another typical answer is more complex. It lists the myriad mistakes made by Russian leaders: allowing "piratization" instead of privatization; empowering selfish courtiers, thus thoroughly discrediting democracy; failing to build institutions; and focusing on self-enrich- ment. It is followed up by criticism of Western leaders for cozying up first to Yeltsin and later to Putin, while failing to speak the truth to them about the crackdown on communists and nationalists in Moscow in 1993, the war in Chechnya and its atrocities, the flawed presidential elections of 1996, and the restriction of media freedoms and authoritar- ian practices of recent years. This view is right, in principle, but it assumes the impossible: either Russia should have a less self-centered leadership or the West should have elevated principle above its interest, which seldom happens in relations with major countries.

Some Russians blame specific Western actions (or inaction) for the failure of the relationship. Among the objectionable actions, two stand out. At the top of the list is the enlargement of NATO, which Russian liberals interpreted as a Western vote of no confidence in Russia's fledgling democracy, and Russian traditionalists as the victorious West's collecting its trophies from victory in the Cold War. Second is the NATO air war on Serbia, read as a sign that the West is not going to bow to Russia's wishes and takes international law and law enforcement into its own hands when it deems it to be in its self-interest. In reality, neither of these actions was particularly anti-Russian. Since NATO's first enlarge- ment into Central and Eastern Europe, the alliance has expanded even further, without, however, increasing the military threat to Russia. Moscow's overall influence in the region has shrunk considerably, but

NATO's expansion was the result, not the reason for this. As to the Kosovo issue, Moscow's real problem was its inability to play the role it craved, i.e., mediator between the Western countries and the rogue regimes, most of which had been Soviet clients during the Cold War and in which Moscow had managed to preserve some influence. More recently, this was evident in Iraq and, briefly, in North Korea.

Before we look at the consequences of Western inaction it is worth examining what Russia might have done. Things would have played out differently if, for instance, Yeltsin had called a fresh election in the fall of 1991, had a new constitution adopted in 1992, banned former Communist Party functionaries (presumably excluding himself) from holding government jobs, thoroughly purged and reformed the security services, carried out a radical military reform, and buried Lenin's body, still kept in a mausoleum. That might have spurred the reform effort, but it might have also led to a civil war, which was never too far away in 1991–1993.

Things would have developed differently if the West had abolished NATO immediately after the end of the Soviet Union, or, alternatively, if it had invited Russia to join, responding to Yeltsin's somewhat heavy hint in December 1991. The United States might have also received Russia's cooperation on a number of issues, including Iraq and Iran, in exchange for its acquiescence to Moscow's primacy in Russia's immediate neighborhood. But the United States was not interested in such a geopolitical deal.

A brief look at these "might have beens" suggests that alternative courses were not more natural or more probable than the ones actually taken. It also suggests that this discussion is of purely academic interest. It provides no insights and does not deepen one's understanding of real history. Still, there are lessons to be learned from either party's experience. The lessons for the West could be summarized as follows:

Russia matters, for better or for worse. Dismissing it as irrelevant has a cost. Taking Russia seriously requires understanding of where it is and where it is headed. It is best to "read" Russia in terms of its own history. Russia should not be confused with the Soviet Union, although it is clearly saddled with a Soviet legacy. In comparison to its immediate predecessor, the Russian Federation exhibits both historical continuities and discontinuities. The former is evident in, for example, the great-power mentality of its elite; the latter, in its new interest in money and private property.

In the wake of the collapse of communism and the end of Russia's imperial period (not to be confused with great-power status), no fundamental problems exist between Russia and the United States or Russia and the European Union. There are real differences of interest, of perception, and of culture (within the common civilization). The value gap is, above all, a reflection of different stages in development between Russian capitalism and present-day Western societies.

Russia cannot be modernized ("Westernized") by means of institutional integration into the West, like Poland or, theoretically, even Ukraine. Not only is it too big, too complex, and in many ways too backward. Its elite is too rigid in its attachment to great-power thinking. Russia wants to be, not so much to belong. The only way forward for Russia is to try to Westernize itself, freely, at its own pace and outside of formal supranational structures. In kind, but not in degree or methods, this is an enterprise comparable to the Meiji revolution in Japan and to the Atatürk reforms in Turkey. In the contemporary world, China's evolution offers some striking parallels to Russia's.

Whether Russia will be able to do this depends on the Russians themselves. The West will have no major direct influence on Russian domestic developments, although its indirect influence, its soft power, will remain enormous. The proximity effect of the European Union on Russia's evolution cannot be overestimated. Seeing the former East Germany turn into eastern Germany was one thing: Germans, east or west, are Germans. Watching the Czech Republic, Hungary, and Poland advance toward Western standards sent a more powerful message and set an example. The success of the Baltic states, with their large Russian minorities, will enhance the message. Most of all, should Ukraine succeed in establishing and practicing real political pluralism, free media, and an independent judiciary, this will be very good news for Russia as a whole, encouraging it to move forward.

Russian–Western relations are competitive and cooperative. With the United States, the former currently prevails, with the EU, the latter. The fundamental problem in the relationship, above and beyond the specific issues, are the terms of engagement. The United States and the EU, in their different ways, do not accept moral equality with Russia and want it to play by their rules. The Russians, for their part, want to get their way, and on their own terms. Russia will not become a junior partner to the United States, nor a mere "associate" of Europe. In order to have productive relationships, Americans and Europeans need to cut back on preaching to Russia to change its ways, and to focus instead on their own interests.

The lessons for Russia from post-Cold War history would include: There is no unique Russian way in the world. To be successful, Russia needs to become modern, i.e., Western. Russia needs modern institutions. It is certainly ready for securing property rights, empowering the judiciary, and starting to establish the rule of law. This is the *ultimate* comparative advantage, incomparably more important than oil and gas or nukes and tanks. This is also the way that leading emerging economies, otherwise known collectively as BRIC (Brazil, Russia, India, China), are going. All basically move in one direction. Each one is special; no one is unique. It would be naïve, of course, to expect Russia to move ahead smoothly and briskly. In fact, the opposite is likely to be true: major political crises are virtually unavoidable in the medium term.

The twenty-first century West is not a bloc but a system of institutions. It includes countries with vastly different cultures. Westernization is not a threat to whatever passes for "Russia's soul"; it is in no danger of being hijacked. The "Euro–Atlantic" West of the EU and NATO is not inherently anti-Russian. Russia is not the central foreign policy issue for either the United States or the European Union. It should disabuse itself of the notion that America and Europe wish it ill and seek its demise and destruction. Instead, Russians need to figure out how engaging the various members of the Euro–Atlantic community properly would promote Russia's modernization, help its fuller integration into the global community, and help guarantee its security.

Russians need to see that "Western values" are not only a big stick that editorial writers carry about, but also a real measure of societal progress. They need to see that while the foundation of Russia's foreign policy (i.e., real and mostly private economic interests) has been established, this policy lacks a spine, which only deeply held values can form. Flexibility and pragmatism have their uses, but they also have major limitations. Cynicism may be striking, but it does not impress. Russia does not have an image problem. It has problems that reflect upon its image.

Russia needs strong relations with the United States to promote domestic modernization, achieve full global integration, and help maintain a secure global and regional environment. Russia needs solid links with the European Union for these same reasons, plus the EU is a close neighbor and potentially a reliable partner.

Conclusion

Russia is a country of big distances and a very long history, one made for long-distance runners. There is an obvious need for a long-term strategy toward Russia, as part of the U.S. global governance project and of the EU's global ascendancy bid.

There is added value in a coordinated strategy between the EU and the United States, but only if the proper balance is struck. Unlike in Cold War days, this cannot be an American-dominated process. The Europeans will have an equal say. A good cop–bad cop division of labor between Europe and America is probably impossible, due to their real differences of interest, even within the European Union, and the hybrid (nation states with the Union superstructure) nature of the EU.

An assessment of where Russia is and where it is headed is key. The notions of a "Weimar Russia" or "Russian fascism" and imperial revanchism, should they become accepted at face value and allowed to inform policy, would exacerbate Russian–Western tensions and lead to conflicts, above all in Georgia and possibly Ukraine. In 1999, with Yeltsin still in the Kremlin, an armed clash was narrowly avoided in Kosovo. At this writing in 2007, a sudden "unfreezing" of ethnic conflict in Georgia could lead to Russia's direct involvement and Georgia's appeal to the United States and NATO for help. If the United States were to attack Iran, this would put the U.S.–Russia relationship to a severe test.

Neither the West nor Russia should allow itself to be used by its clients or would-be friends. Moscow had bad experience with its late "friends" in Belgrade and Baghdad, Milosevic and Hussein. It should be careful with the rulers in Tehran, Pyongyang, Havana, and Minsk. America and Europe need to appreciate that, like any formerly dominant nation Russia faces a number of countries that view it through the prism of their historical experience. This wariness is understandable and the tensions are real. Some of these countries are EU members and NATO allies and deserve reassurance and support. However, what the United States and the EU should guard against is being exploited by Russia's neighbors as a vehicle to settle old scores against the former imperial center.

In a practical way, Russia needs to be rediscovered. At present, Western publics show an overwhelming interest in China and India.

Meanwhile, their governments are preoccupied with the Middle East and related problems, such as terrorism, Islamist activism, and WMD proliferation. Russia slips through the net and gets stereotyped, which distorts the Western outlook and damages Western policies. The U.S. and EU governments require a new paradigm for dealing with Russia, one squarely based on Western values but clearly geared to American and European interests. This paradigm and its implications will be laid out in the concluding chapter.

CONCLUSION

THE CASE FOR A PARADIGM SHIFT. RUSSIA AS A NEW WEST

U.S. and European elites still think of Russia in terms of the 1990s and apply the democracy paradigm to it. No wonder what they see is a failed democracy. This is strikingly different from the way communist China is now being viewed, not to mention India. Russia today is seen in stark contrast to postwar Germany and Japan or postcommunist Ukraine and Georgia, even Kazakhstan, and, of course, to the post-1991 vision of Russia itself. In a world where the United States and Europe enjoy good relations with all other major emerging powers, Putin's Russia, in the Western public mind, joins Iran, Syria, North Korea, Cuba, Venezuela, and Zimbabwe as a reviled regime. A resurgent, even revanchist Russia is turning into a cliché, evoking uncomfortable parallels with Weimar Germany.

There are two schools of thought behind this approach. One believes that Russia continues to be a declining power, increasingly irrelevant to the United States, and thus does not merit much attention. Good riddance, in the eyes of proponents of this view: a world without Russia would be a safer world. The other is worried about Russia's newfound assertiveness, even aggressiveness, which threatens certain sensitive international markets (such as energy and weapons trade). From this school's perspective, Russia needs to be opposed and boxed in. Both views are essentially negative and would merge under the heading: Russia is not so much an emerging market as an emerging threat.

This perspective is wrong, but not because it is unkind. It is wrong because it is emotional and distorted. Moreover, it is dangerous because it is disorienting. It seeks to add Russia hastily to the impressive list of problems U.S. policies are encountering and risks overloading the agenda and tipping the balance against American and European interests. It provokes in Russia exactly the kind of response it purports to protect the West from: an attempt to revisit the ending of the Cold War. The payoff for such an approach is nowhere to be seen.

As the United States proceeds to rethink its foreign and security policy in the wake of the Iraq experience, it needs a new global outlook. Any ideological bent is inherently distorting, for it turns invariably complex reality into a simple caricature of itself. The *ideology* of democracy promotion is no exception. This does not negate the practical need to help democracy succeed authoritarianism, but ideology is usually an impractical tool toward that end.

Americans and Europeans are right in their analysis of the rise of the new powers, led by China and India. They should be specially commended for welcoming that rise (especially China's), and not conspiring to retard and check it. The fact that, in public opinion and especially among the business community, China enjoys goodwill in the West is hugely fortunate. This does not mean, however, that the gradual change in the distribution of power and influence in the world will be no problem for America, Europe, and Japan. Peaceful and amicable relations among the principal powers, which are historically unprecedented, should not be taken for granted.

This is not a call for pre-emptive coalition-building against potential adversaries. To the contrary, while the United States continues to tower over the rest of the world, it would be wise to go beyond its current role of the most powerful nation state, adding the function of the leader of the international system, a kind of CEO of World, Inc. The United States can accomplish many things single-handedly, but there is a limit to what even the world's premier power can achieve. The United Nations, on the other hand, has universal representation and a unique cachet of legitimacy, but it is a platform, rather than a player.

The principal international issue in the post-Iraq world will be that of world governance. Global warming and international terrorism, proliferation of weapons of mass destruction, the failure of many states to perform their basic functions (failed states), trade and development: all these global issues, plus a number of regional ones, starting with the conflicts in the Greater Middle East, demand efficient and effective management.

The way to come to grips with these issues is not by creating an alliance of democracies. The selection process will inevitably be awkward, the result inconsistent, and the impact divisive. Of course, the United States and the European Union need to further cement their historical ties, and NATO should find a formula to cooperate with its partners in East Asia and Oceania. Neither of these alliances, however, is fully global. The truly winning and forward-looking formula is not the spread of democracy but the expansion of the West.

Chapter 2 provided an outline of the evolution of the concept of the West, from its early Anglo-American beginnings to the Cold War and then post-Cold War West. Its further expansion, as the Russian case has richly demonstrated, cannot proceed in institutionalized forms. There is a limit to EU enlargement and to NATO membership.

Yet if one looks at China, India, and Brazil, or Argentina and South Africa, or Indonesia and Kazakhstan, what one sees is the expansion and entrenchment of Western ways and institutions. The emerging markets around the world stand for nothing but a new West *in potential*. The aspiring capitalists of Asia, Latin America, Africa, and Eastern Europe follow, albeit under vastly different domestic and external conditions, the road that others before them have trodden. The remainder of the "second world" and the leaders of the third one are actually following in the footsteps of the first. Francis Fukuyama was right, after all, in the sense of the totality of victory in the Cold War. Only it was a victory for the capitalist roaders, and not yet for democracy.

With few exceptions, India being the most notable one, the westernizing nations are not mature democracies. Unless they manage to build political institutions, which are the essence of the West, they will fail dismally. One cannot hope to confine reforms to the economic sphere: capitalist development absolutely requires securing property rights and establishing the rule of law. Consumer society, by internalizing the freedom of choice in goods and services, prepares the ground for the expansion of that freedom beyond the realms of economy and entertainment. Consumers are citizens-in-waiting. People's capitalism creates stakeholders in the system and breeds responsibility. As society changes, so do its values. However, it is interests that are the true engines of change.

The emerging New West nominally accounts for the majority of the world's population, although in reality only the middle classes and the elites are becoming westernized in practice. Yet therein lies the hope not only for the existing West, which thus won't be swamped by "the Rest," but for humanity as a whole. To the extent that the new Westerners turn into stakeholders of the international system, peace, stability and prosperity in the twenty-first century will be assured. Eventually, capitalism will lead to some form of representative government and a democratic polity. It is the global promotion of liberalism and modernization, rather than that of democracy, that should be the centerpiece of Western foreign policy.

That should not be lost on American and European politicians as they ponder the experience of Iraq. Global governance should be the natural focus of their efforts. Issues such as nuclear proliferation, climate change, energy security, and aid to modernization call for joint efforts of key international players. Trying to go it alone will lead to failure and isolation. Postponing efforts to assume true global leadership in cooperation with other centers of power would only weaken America's and Europe's claim to lead: the New West is growing at a faster pace than the Old, and its self-confidence is rising. Inclusiveness can win the day; exclusiveness will ruin the future.

Russia can make it to the New West. It is not so much continuing in decline as being reconstituted. The end of the empire and of the communist system eliminated a major burden to its development, even though the end of both came at a huge price. Today, its economy is not all oil, gas, and metals. The market is a reality in Russia, albeit in a very primitive and grossly distorted form. The middle class is small, but growing, as rising personal incomes approach those of some of the EU's east-central European members.

Politically, Russia is still an autocracy, presided over by a czarist president. His subjects show little interest in politics and will ratify the leader's choice of a successor, whoever the candidate is. However, this apathy, which puts so many Russian liberals in despair, has a silver lining. Most Russians want to be left alone by the state. They do not bother and do not want to be bothered. They leave politics, i.e., clan struggle, to their nominal leaders, as they go about their own business. By taking care of themselves and leaving "Russia" to the elites for the time being, they are, in fact, building a material foundation for the next step. Over time, Russia will acquire more and more rightful owners: from a few dozen today to a few hundred several years from now to hundreds of thousands. Within a generation, having a single master of the land will first become impossible and then unthinkable. The powers of government will have to be separated in reality, not just on paper. A need for checks and balances will naturally emerge. Governance and competence are likely to emerge as criteria for grading the political regime and determining its fate. Russia circa 2025 will still not be a democracy, but it will be considerably more liberal and modern. The liberalism that has a chance to prevail in Russia will be economically driven.

American and European foreign policy should seek to strengthen the forces of liberalism and modernization in Russia. Market forces can be relied upon to open up Russia even wider and help transform it even more deeply, but they need encouragement. Russia's forthcoming entry into the World Trade Organization is a hugely important transformative step. Once Russia is fully integrated into the world economy, it will become accustomed to international capitalist norms and practices, including court arbitration. The need for a modern legal system in Russia itself will become not merely obvious, but truly compelling. Moscow has now set its sights on joining the Organisation for Economic Co-operation and Development (OECD), which, when it comes, will be a symbolic certificate of its graduation from economic transition. Full integration will take a long time, but every step along that way will create new positive realities, not merely in the Russian economy, but also in society at large and, ultimately, in the Russian polity.

The United States and the EU would be wise to allow Russian compa- nies (whether private or majority state-owned) to enter Western markets without unreasonable restrictions. Of course, they need to make sure that these companies conform to the existing rules and norms, learn to benefit from them, and thus become their supporters. Russians want their designated national champions to enter the Top Ten company lists, in terms of capitalization, in a number of fields, starting with raw materi- als. They want those companies to become transnational, too. This requires transparency, accountability, and good corporate governance: all the essential ingredients for successful IPOs and subsequent competition on the global market. The Russian bid is hardly a threat to others: Russia is unlikely to take over the world economy or even its key sectors. Rather, it is a way for the Russians to improve their business culture, and be rewarded by a surge in capitalization and profits.

Fostering economic interdependence is the best way of creating solid links between Russia and the European Union and Russia and the United States. Holding Russian companies to normal Western standards of corporate practices is key. Good governance and prosperity will become more firmly and more widely established, since they are intimately linked to competitiveness and profitability. Under these conditions, for Americans and Europeans owning a piece of Russia and allowing Russian companies to own assets in their own countries would bring both profit and reassurance to all interested parties. An early repeal of the largely symbolic relics of the past, such as the Jackson-Vanik Amendment, and giving Russia permanent normal trade relations (PNTR) status would help U.S. businesses dealing with Russia and create a general climate more propitious for bilateral economic exchanges.

Western businesses, which are expanding their activities in Russia, are working models of advance governance and culture. Through their presence they also generate competition and improve market conditions in the country. The recent moves by the Kremlin to limit foreign participation in the energy industry, heavy-handed as they are, do not signal a reversal in the government policy of attracting foreign investment. First, energy, regarded as the crown jewel, is a special case. At the other extreme, the Russian car industry has been virtually turned over to foreign companies. Second, even though Russia may be awash with money at the moment, it badly needs advanced technology and best business practices.

Company-level integration, in which Russian and Western partners engage in equity swaps, leads to internationalizing the Russian business outlook. The rise of multinationals with Russian equity capital would take Russian capitalism to a new plane. That will have implications for Moscow's foreign policy by requiring a much wider outlook and providing the perspective of a vested insider rather than an outsider creating problems to get attention.

Political moderation on Russia's part can be encouraged by closer cooperation with the United States and Europe on global issues. Russia's dissenting views on Iran and North Korea are not wholly determined by its commercial interests. There is some value to Moscow's long and varied historical experience with Tehran and to its insights. A Moscow that can and will say no to certain approaches within Western countries, such as the use of force, can be a useful partner in crafting more sophisticated policies, ones with a better chance of success. The same can be said for North Korea, where Washington prefers to deal with Beijing as its principal partner (which is right), barely tolerating Moscow (which is wrong).

Energy links, which were touted in 2001–2003 as the material foundation for U.S.–Russian and EU–Russian strategic partnerships, have since become a source of tension. Yet a closer look at Gazprom practices suggests that the principal objective its managers have in mind is enhancing the company's profits and raising its net worth. This is often done clumsily, at a high cost to Russia's political interests and the country's image abroad. True, the fact that there is no world price for natural gas does allow the Russian government to manipulate prices to suit its political interests. However, the hard reality remains: a typical "energy weapon" is usually linked to subsidies and discounts. A full price, which Western customers pay, always comes without strings attached.

Russians are seeking to enter West European and, eventually, U.S. energy markets and to acquire downstream assets, including distribution networks, to make greater profits. They also want to ensure what they call "the security of demand," i.e., long-term contracts or, even better, a foothold in the retail market. Europe needs to overcome its ancient fears and accept interdependence with Russia. Moscow depends far more on the proceeds from Russian companies' energy sales to Europe (two-thirds of its total foreign exchange revenue), than the EU countries do on their Russian gas imports (around 25 percent). Achieving a proper balance of interests between the Russian producers and the EU consumers would mean hard bargaining on both sides, but eventually this would necessitate opening on both sides. The United States, for its part, would do well to integrate the Russian nuclear industry, which is on the verge of becoming an "Atomprom," into a global system that would ensure high nonproliferation standards.

On climate change, Russia has long since ratified the Kyoto Protocol, even if acceptance was part of a global deal struck with the EU on the way to becoming a WTO member. Russia, which is particularly well endowed with such valuable resources as fresh water and forests, is a natural partner for solving global ecological issues.

Will the Russians cooperate with America, Europe, and others on global governance issues? Probably "yes," but the real question is, on what terms. They want their great-power status confirmed, and being a member of a "global ruling politburo" (i.e., the G8) as well as the world's legislating "central committee" (the UN Security Council) is their ambition. Extending the Soviet-era analogy a bit further, one might say Moscow wants to be both the secretary of energy and secretary for ideology. The Russians clearly prefer being influential insiders rather than disgruntled outsiders. Actually, they share many key interests with their Western partners. However, they have their own perspective and should not be expected to follow others automatically. They will seek to promote their interests and minimize their concessions. Of course, there is a confidence gap between them and their would-be partners. A modicum of good faith needs to be established before any party can move forward. This will not be easy, but there is a way.

Winston Churchill, in referring to Russia as a riddle inside an enigma, conceded that there was, perhaps, a way of dealing with it. He called it the Russian national interest. It is a matter for discussion to what extent the *national* interest exists in contemporary Russia, but the various subnational interests (clan, corporate, and personal—all essentially private) reign supreme. While the national interest will take some time to develop—it will be a function of Russia's turning itself into a nation by forming the stabilizing bedrock of a middle class—group vested interests are in evidence today. Anyone serious about dealing with Russia must learn to address them.

Interests change people's behavior and even people themselves. Members of the Russian elite have been actively engaged in what may be called "individual integration" into international business and society circles. Mikhail Khodorkovsky was prescient enough to see this ahead of others. He found a way to transform his reputation, in a Saul-to-Paul manner, in a matter of a few years. He did not err there. His failure was wholly due to his misjudgment and miscalculation in managing relations with the Kremlin. Now, with Khodorkovsky in jail, even his detractors are following in his footsteps in seeking to embellish their reputations in the West. Few are acquiring fancy yachts in order to sail the Arctic Ocean. Still fewer want to land in jail while visiting America or Switzerland. Although they almost never come into the public view, the personal interests of the people who "both rule Russia and own it," especially if that number grows substantially, can be a major stabilizing force in the Russian–Western relationship.

This constellation of interests at the top is not trivial, but it is the expansion of the role of the middle classes that has the potential to normalize Russian–Western relations by projecting those relations far beyond the government and corporate world. For Russian mid-level and small entrepreneurs to engage fully with the West, they need a friendlier visa regime with the United States and EU countries. The Russian government has to demonstrate that it is steadily improving the country's immigration and border-crossing regime as well as the quality of travel documents, such as passports. But there is hardly a case for the perennial threat of "hordes of Russians swarming into the EU." This did not happen in 1991 and is unlikely to happen in the future. To the extent that Russians would be leaving emigration is more likely to benefit the EU than damage it.

On humanitarian matters, members of the Council of Europe have a right and an obligation to hold the Russian Federation responsible for its commitments. However, the Europeans need to be ready to respond to Russian charges of bias, double standards, and unequal treatment. They also need to remember that several other former Soviet states, some of them currently with friendlier ties to the West than Russia, exhibit similar flaws when it comes to human rights. True, Russia bears a special responsibility to the international community as a permanent member of the UN Security Council. Yet, politicizing the situation could result in Moscow's withdrawing its support from the Council of Europe and losing interest in the Organization for Security and Co-operation in Europe. It is better to let the international courts tackle individual cases and pass judgment. This would also, indirectly, enhance the role of the judiciary inside Russia.

The issue of the G8 is particularly sensitive. As this book argues, Russia's membership, granted in 1998, was the product of diplomatic expediency at the time rather than a recognition of Russia's progress. However, expelling Russia and going back to an all-Western G7 carries a major and unnecessary risk. Moscow would interpret excommunication as a hostile act. Russia's foreign policy would turn overtly anti-American, and Moscow would feel the need to found or join a rival club. This would not make things easier for the United States. A Cold War of choice is unlikely to benefit either Russia or the West.

Yet there is a problem with the G8, which obviously lacks homogeneity. An all-Western club of choice did lose its coherence and character through admission of a country that neither qualified for nor really deserved its membership. This could be addressed by enlarging the body to a world-governance G-X (-12, -14) by inviting emerging economies, such as China, India, Brazil, South Africa, and possibly a few others. This group would function as the world's informal governing board and develop solutions that would be formally approved by the

UN Security Council. If the United States chose to act not only as the world's lone superpower but also as the equivalent of the CEO in World, Inc., it would find the "World's Board" a useful partner in global governance. As for "members of the board," they would learn to share the burden of governance and become, in the words of Robert Zoellick, "responsible stakeholders" in the international system. It could be that the United States, EU, and Japan would rediscover a smaller old Western club. For their part, China, India, Russia, and Brazil (also known as BRIC) are already on their way to institutionalizing their meetings at three and four members.

The EU needs its own strategic approach to Russia. The Russia Federation will not be a member of the European Union, but it can become a major partner, sharing a continent with the EU. The 2005 road map of EU–Russian partnership is a sound statement of intent and needs to be filled with practical projects. Priority setting is key. Transport infrastructure development is an obvious top candidate, with Russian roads, railways, airports, and port facilities requiring massive overhaul, improvement, and expansion. When upgraded and developed, they will add materially to the EU's capability to project its products and services across Eurasia.

With relations between the new members of the European Union, especially the Baltic States and Poland, on the one hand, and Russia, on the other, having turned into an area of constant tension, the Union can ill afford to deny solidarity to Central and Eastern Europeans. Solidarity means mutual support *and* shared responsibility: the EU has both to respond to Russia and answer to its members.

It is important for both Europe and the United States to avoid being drawn too deeply into geopolitical gaming in the former Soviet Union. Competition for power and influence among the major powers cannot be uninvented, but unlike in the nineteenth century, the future of the new states that have emerged from the Soviet Union will largely depend on these states themselves, not on Washington, Brussels, Beijing, or Moscow. The larger of these states, such as Ukraine, Kazakhstan, and Uzbekistan, will define their orientation based on their domestic situation, cultural affinities, and perceived international identities. Essentially, this will be about the choices made by the local elites and the degree of transformation of their societies. No one from the outside will "own" the former imperial borderlands.

Of course, the West would do best to focus on helping domestic reform in the new countries. In particular, Ukraine's success with reforming its economy and governance would have an enormously positive effect on Russia. Ukraine, thanks to its size and its significant body of Russian speakers, is in many ways an "alternative Russia," capable of projecting positive influence not only to the Russian Federation, but also to Belarus, Kazakhstan, and other parts of the post-Soviet Commonwealth. Helping Ukraine to reform and rise is a hugely important thing in its own right, but it would also contribute greatly to the success of U.S. and EU policies toward Russia. One thing is certain, of course: The best way to make reforms in Ukraine irreversible is for the EU to offer that country a clear perspective of membership, even in the time frame of fifteen years or more.

One reason why Ukraine is so critical is that, for many Russians, it is another country, but not really a foreign one. In a way, helping Ukraine succeed would get a handle on Russian domestic developments. At the same time, the West should avoid becoming involved in Russia's internal politics. Becoming enamored of Russian leaders or charmed by the avowedly pro-Western dissidents could be as futile and dangerous as demonizing the former and dismissing the latter. The Western approach in general needs to be squarely based on interests, succumbing neither to wishful thinking nor self-fulfilling prophecies.

NATO enlargement should not become a low-cost substitute for European integration. Western leaders need to be careful lest the NATO issue lead to a dangerous split within national societies, as it could in Ukraine. In Georgia, by contrast, the entire elite supports NATO membership, but the allies need to think carefully about the impact of Georgia's entry for the prospects of conflict resolution in Abkhazia and South Ossetia and for relations between the West and Russia. The fact that Russia has no veto in the matter does not mean that there will be no impact. The core interest of America and Europe lies in Russia's living peacefully with its neighbors within recognized borders.

The energy relations between Russia and the new states, while tense, are now resting on a firmer footing of commercial interest. Paradoxical as it may seem, Gazprom's raising of prices in 2005–2007 proved an act of liberation of the CIS states, which have since owed the Russians nothing but money in exchange for the energy they consume. More than anything else, this step has set the former Soviet Union on the path of the USSR itself. Special ties among the ex-Soviet republics are being fast replaced by more conventional relations based on commercial considerations. Gazprom's tough policies have also created an incentive for wide-ranging industrial reforms in the countries concerned.

As far as the frozen conflicts are concerned, the impact of the Kosovo situation does reverberate from Transnistria to the Caucasus. Actually, the string of unresolved conflicts in Europe and Asia is very long, posing a set of challenges to world powers. For many of these conflicts to be managed and helped toward eventual resolution, the United States and the EU will need Russia's cooperation. Moldova/Transnistria is a good place to start and establish a much-needed precedent of successful conflict resolution.

To sum up: The task of American statesmen is not so much to consolidate the Old West as to expand it at the margins. It is to reach out to the New West, while America is still at the peak of its power, and offer it a deal.

America and Europe need to look at Russia as an emerging capitalist society, rather than a failed democratic polity. They would understand Russia better if they used the vocabulary of practical economics, rather than of political science. They would have no more sincere friends in Russia than people wishing to do business with the West. When Russia's principal business becomes defined as just business, as President William Harding once famously said about America, the country will be ready to move to another station on its postcommunist adventure. This station will still not be called "Democracy," but it may sound like "the Rule of Law," with a transfer to "Constitutional Government." This won't make dealing with Russia always a pleasure, but it will make for a much more predictable and productive future. After so many failures and false starts in the decade and a half since the end of the Soviet Union, getting, and then *doing* Russia right, for once, would not only be a good thing in itself. It would help create a better world.

INDEX

health and well-being of the
people, 26–27
rise of nationalism, 27–28
NATO (North Atlantic Treaty Organization), xi, 40–41, 84
air-war on Serbia, 85, 93
Bosnia-Hercegovina peacekeeping
operation, 92
Cold War origins, 38–39
eastward expansion, 31–33, 41,
43–44, 47, 71, 72, 85–86, 90,
93–94
Kosovo intervention, 41, 71, 72, 85,
86, 90
Russia's application for membership, 70, 71, 73–75
war on terrorism, 43–44, 90–91
NATO–Russia Council (NRC), 90
NATO–Russia Founding Act, 71, 90
Naumann Foundation, 88
Nazism, 36–37, 48, 65–66
neo-Eurasianism, 73–75
new paradigm for understanding
Russia, xi–xii, 4–7, 28–29
capitalism as mechanism for
reform, 45–48, 103–9
cooperation and competition with
the West, 95–98
failure of democracy promotion
paradigms, xi, 76, 101–2, 112
practical economics, 101–12
regional conflict resolution, 112
See also future of Russia
the New West, xi, 46–48, 103–4, 112
Nicholas I, czar of Russia, 61–62, 63
nongovernmental organizations
(NGOs), 3
North American Free Trade Association (NAFTA), 40
North Atlantic Cooperation Council
(NACC), 70
North Atlantic Treaty Organization
(NATO). See NATO
Northern War, 54, 59
North Korea, 72, 74, 95, 106–7
Novgorod, 53, 55
NTV, 20

Occident. See Europe
oligarchs, 1, 93
emergence under Yeltsin, 10, 22
energy industry. See energy
industry
individual integration, 108
openness, x, 17–18, 19
The Open Society Institute, 88
Ordin-Nashchokin, Afanasy, 56
Organisation for Economic Cooperation and Development
(OECD), 39, 44, 105
Organization for Security and Cooperation in Europe (OSCE), 4, 46,
72, 74, 109
Ostpolitik, 80

Palestinian territories, 42
Patriarch of Moscow, 56
patriotism, 18, 27
perestroika, 3, 20–21, 67–68, 79–83
Persian Gulf War, 83
Peter the Great, czar of Russia, 54,
59, 61
Pipes, Richard, 20
Politkovskaya, Anna, 3
Poland
Community of Democratic Choice,
32
EU membership, 4, 32
historical overview, 36, 55, 59, 61
independence from the Soviet
Union, 82
Pope John Paul II, 80
modernization, 95
NATO membership, 72
quality of life measures, 15, 25
relations with Russia, 110
war on terrorism, 43
political system, x, 104–5
czarism of Putin, x, 9–10, 104–5
institution building and reform, 47–
48, 103–9
political activism, 23–24
political parties, 10
population demographics
decline, 26

immigration, 27
life expectancy, 27
per capita GDP, 15–16, 47
Portugal, 39
post-Cold-War era, 40–46
foreign policies of Russia. *See*
foreign policies of Russia
Western policies towards Russia.
See Western policies towards
Russia
postimperialism, 75
Powell, Colin, 20
Pozharsky, Dmitri, 54
Prague coup, 38
Primakov, Evgenii, 63
private property rights, 13–15, 22, 28,
35, 62, 87, 103–4
prosecutor general, 9
provincial growth and development,
16–17
Pskov, 53
public utilities, 24
Putin (Vladimir) administration, 2–4,
10–11, 18
Beslan terrorist attack, 2, 65
Chechnya war, 76
Conventional Forces in Europe
treaty, 61
czarist style, x, 9–10, 104–5
economic reforms, 45–48, 103–9
nationalist slogans of, 28
recentralization of power, 2–3
Shanghai Cooperation Organization, 3, 72–75
succession concerns, 10, 22
Western support, 93

Reagan (Ronald) administration, 67–
68, 79–81
regional growth and development,
16–17
relations with the West. *See* foreign
policies
religious freedom, 18–19
See also Russian Orthodox Church
(ROC)
REN-TV, 20

Reykjavik summit of 1986, 80–81
Rio Pact, 39
Romania, 45
Roosevelt, Franklin Delano, 65
Rosneft, 14
RTVi, 20
rule of law promotion, xii, 28, 35, 103–
4
Russian Orthodox Church (ROC), 18–
19, 25, 51–52, 56
Russian Union of Industrialists and
Entrepreneurs (RSPP), 22
Russia's Wrong Track (Council on
Foreign Relations), 93

Satarov, Georgi, 10
Sberbank, 14
Scowcroft, Brent, 20
security services, 3, 18
separation of powers, 9
September 11, 2001 terrorist attacks,
2, 90
Serbia, 33, 44, 72, 97
EU aspirations, 45
NATO air-war on, 85, 93
Sergiev Posad, 16–17
Shanghai Cooperation Organization
(SCO), 3, 72–75
Shevardnadze, Eduard, 44, 81
Shevtsova, Lilia, 11
Single European Act, 40
social system, x
abolition of serfdom, 60–61
historical overview, 60–63
middle class, 23–24, 104, 108
oligarchs, 1, 10, 22, 93, 108
transformation of values, 21
Soldiers' Mothers, 88
South Africa, 41, 75, 103
Southeast Asia Treaty Organization
(SEATO), 39
South Korea, 46
South Ossetia, 26, 111
Soviet Union
Afghanistan war, 44, 57, 80–81
arms reduction treaties, 83
Cold War, 38–40, 57–59, 64, 66–68

collapse and breakup, 40, 67–68, 83
Communist Party losses under
  Gorbachev, 81
Eurasianism, 73
Gorbachev's era of *perestroika,*
  79–83
isolationist policies, 64–68
military superpower status of, 58–
  59
policies towards the West, 51–68
Reykjavik summit of 1986, 80–81
Western policies towards, 79–83
World War II, 37–38
Spain, 39
St. Petersburg, 53, 60
Stalin (Joseph) administration, 38,
  65–66
  Cold War, 38–40, 57–59, 64, 66–68
  economic policies, 12
  property rights, 13
Stolypin, Pyotr, 62
Strategic Arms Reduction treaties, 83
Supreme Soviet, 1
Suvorov, Victor, 20
Sweden, 39, 54, 55, 59, 61
Switzerland, 39

Taiwan, 46
Talbott, Strobe, 20
terrorism, 41–44, 90–91, 102–3
  Beslan terrorist attack, 2, 65
  September 11, 2001 terrorist
    attacks, 2, 90
Thatcher, Margaret, 68, 80
Transnistria, 26, 76, 112
travel, 19
Treaty of Rapallo, 57
Treaty of Rome, 38
Treaty of Versailles of 1919, 36
Trotsky, Leon, 63
Truman, Harry, 38, 65
Tunisia, 46
Turkey, 61, 95
  Atatürk's reforms, 33, 47, 95
  democratization process, 43
  EU aspirations, 33, 45
  Europeanization process, 39–40

NATO membership, 39
TV-6, 20

Ukraine
  ethnic Russians, 26
  EU aspirations, 45
  future of, 110–11
  NATO and EU aspirations, 32–33,
    111
  Orange Revolution of 2004, 3, 32,
    44
  quality of life measures, 15
  Russian gas pipeline shutdown, 3,
    92
  war on terrorism, 43, 52–53, 69, 71,
    95, 97
Union of Right Forces (SPS), 10
United Nations, xii, 3–4, 74, 102
United Russia party, 10
United States, 4
  arms reduction treaties, 83
  CEO role in world governance,
    102–3, 110
  Cold War, 38–40, 57–59, 64, 66–68
  Cox Commission Report, 92–93
  democracy promotion policies, 42–
    43
  economic cooperation agreements
    with Russia, 91
  future relations with Russia, 95–98
  Iran policies, 97
  Iraq war, 2, 42–43, 95, 102
  League of Nations, 37
  Malta summit of 1989, 82–83
  Marshall Plan, 38
  post-Cold-War era, 40–46, 72, 76
  Reagan administration policies,
    67–68, 79
  regional alliances, 38–39
  Reykjavik summit of 1986, 80–81
  Russian policies towards. *See*
    foreign policies of Russia
  September 11, 2001 terrorist
    attacks, 2, 90
  War of Independence, 59
  war on terrorism, 41–42, 43, 90–91

See also Western policies towards Russia

U.S.S.R. *See* Soviet Union

utilities, 24
See also energy industry

Uzbekistan, 3, 71, 110

values gap, 47–48

Vladimir, prince of Kiev, 52

VTB, 14

war on terrorism, 41–42, 43, 90–91

Warsaw Pact, 31

Washington Consensus, 87, 89

Western Christianity, 18–19

Westernization, 31–35
  core principles of, 35
  democratization, 36
  expansion of capitalism, 35, 47–48
  the New West, xi, 46–48, 103–4, 112
  participation in Europe, 29–33
  See also Europe

Westernization of Russia. *See* new paradigm for understanding Russia

Western policies towards Russia, 5–6, 48, 79, 84–98
  association instead of integration, 84, 89–92
  creation of civil society and NGOs, 87–89
  decline management, 84–86
  economic and financial advice, 87
  economic cooperation agreements, 91
  economic loans, 81–82
  energy partnerships, 91–92
  expansion of NATO and the EU, 85–86, 90
  failures and future options, 92–98
  humanitarian support, 86–87
  NATO-Russia Founding Act, 71, 90
  participation in Western markets, 105–6, 108–9
  rejection of Russia's quest for equality, 70, 71, 73–75, 96

summit diplomacy, 80–81, 82–83, 90

support for Yeltsin, 85, 93

transformation assistance, 84, 86–89

war on terrorism, 41–42, 43, 90–91

Western policies towards the Soviet Union, 79–83

West Germany. *See* Germany

Wilson, Woodrow, 36

Witte, Sergei, 25, 63

WMD proliferation, 84–86, 103

World Bank, 70

World Trade Organization (WTO), xii, 24, 91, 105, 107

World War I, 35–36, 48, 55, 60, 66

World War II, 36–38, 48, 55, 59, 64–66

Yabloko party, 10

Yakovlev, Alexander, 81

Yeltsin (Boris) administration, 1
  application for membership in NATO, 70, 71
  Chechnya war, 1, 18, 72, 76, 85, 93
  claims of victory in the Cold War, 69–70
  collapse of the Soviet Union, 83
  Council of Europe membership, 72
  crackdowns of 1993, 93
  election of 1996, 85, 93
  integration and assimilation goals, 25–26
  Kosovo intervention, 92, 94, 97
  Kozyrev line, 70
  role of the oligarchs, 10, 22
  Western support, 85, 93

Yugansk, 14

Yugoslavia, 39

YUKOS business empire, 2, 14, 17, 92

Zhirinovsky, Vladimir, 10, 27–28

Zoelick, Robert, 110

Zyuganov, Gennadi, 27–28

ABOUT THE AUTHOR

Dmitri V. Trenin is deputy director of the Carnegie Moscow Center, a senior associate of the Carnegie Endowment, and co-chair of the Moscow Center's Foreign and Security Policy Program. He has been with the Center since its inception in 1993.

From 1993–1997, Trenin held posts as a senior research fellow at the NATO Defense College in Rome and a senior research fellow at the Institute of Europe in Moscow. He served in the Soviet and Russian armed forces from 1972 to 1993, including experience working as a liaison officer in the External Relations Branch of the Group of Soviet Forces and as a staff member of the delegation to the U.S.–Soviet nuclear arms talks in Geneva from 1985 to 1991. He is the author of *Russia's Restless Frontier: The Chechnya Factor in Post-Soviet Russia* (with Aleksei V. Malashenko) *and The End of Eurasia: Russia on the Border Between Geopolitics and Globalization*, both published by the Carnegie Endowment.